The Secret Word Is
GROUCHO

The Secret Word Is GROUCHO

by Groucho Marx

with Hector Arce

G. P. Putnam's Sons, New York

Endpapers: A montage from the show, YOU BET YOUR LIFE.
(Robert Dwan Collection)

COPYRIGHT © 1976 BY GROUCHO MARX

Second Impression
SBN: 399-11690-7
Library of Congress Catalog
Card Number: 76-458

PRINTED IN THE UNITED STATES OF AMERICA

To THE DUCK

A comedian belongs to the people, but the show in which this one is most often exposed belongs to the National Broadcasting Company. For permission to use frame blow-ups from films of the show, my thanks go to that network's Herbert Schlosser and Tod A. Roberts.

My gratitude also goes to those who offered encouragement on the project and those who shared their memories and memorabilia: Edgar Bergen, my daughter, Melinda Marx Berti, Irving Brecher, Phyllis Diller, Robert Dwan, George Fenneman, Jerry Fielding, Erin Fleming, Hy Freedman, Pedro Gonzalez Gonzalez, John Guedel, Howard Harris, Jack Meakin, Edwin I. Mills, Marion Pollock, Morrie Ryskind, Thomas Wilhite and—especially—Bernie Smith.

Special thanks also go to Steve Stoliar, keeper of the Groucho Marx Archives, and to my grandson, Andy Marx, who monitored dozens of shows to extract the sequences quoted in the Appendix.

I am also grateful to the Los Angeles *Times*, the A.C. Nielsen Company and Virgil Partch for permission to use their material.

And finally, thanks to you and all our contestants.

—GROUCHO

AND NOW, HERE HE IS, THE ONE, THE ONLY—

"THAT'S ME, Groucho Marx!"

Only the most trivial of the trivia collectors would keep score on how many times I spoke that phrase.

Or try this one on for size: "Welcome to *You Bet Your Life.* Say the secret word and divide one hundred dollars. It's a common word, something you see every day."

Only the nittiest of the nitpickers would keep tab on how many contestants I welcomed in this manner. By the way, have you noticed how perfect the words are, how carefully structured they seem?

"All right, here we go for the big question. I'll give you fifteen seconds to decide on a single answer between you. Think carefully and, please, no help from the audience."

It was hard to live up to *that* material, but after fourteen seasons of *You Bet Your Life,* in which I did 500-plus programs and met 2,500 contestants, I think I got the hang of it.

Unlike my brother Chico, I'm not much of a gambler, and spouting off the show's statistics is the only numbers game I'll play . . . unless you want to consider the Nielsen ratings and, believe me, that's not play. Broadcasting empires have been built on their shaky foundation, and have come tumbling down with a misplaced decimal.

Did I say show business is fun and games? Not on your tin-type, and that should give you some understanding of how long *I've* been at it. And am I going to tell you about the agony and the ecstasy of creating the most successful quiz show in television history? You bet your life!

I must admit that the fortunes of the Marx Brothers during those early years of the Second World War were not at their highest.

We hadn't made a movie since 1941, and *The Big Store* to some critics was The Big Bore. Which is a hell of a way to talk about our farewell film. But who are critics to say? Have *you* ever met a critic? They all take cheap shots, except when you're buying the drinks.

Anyway, early in 1942, we announced—again—that after more than thirty years as a team, the Marx Brothers were disbanding. Immediately thereafter, the motion picture industry embarked on a public relations campaign with a theme that "Movies are better than ever." That's gratitude, folks.

I figured if, no matter what I did, I was going to get this much static, there was only one avenue open to me. Radio.

I'd flirted with the idea before, way back in the Early Thirties. Chico and I had done a half-hour radio show called *Flywheel, Shyster and Flywheel* for the Esso Oil Company. We'd moved to New York for the coast-to-coast broadcast. Company sales, as a result of our show, had risen precipitously. Profits doubled in that brief time, and Esso felt guilty taking the money. So Esso dropped us after twenty-six weeks. Those were the days of guilt-edged securities, which don't exist today.

Then, again with Chico, I did a show for Kellogg in 1939. We hired some promising young kids in support: Cary

Grant, Carole Lombard, Madeline Carroll, Lawrence Tibbett, and Basil Rathbone. But they were in way over their heads, and just couldn't cope with success. Rather than replace them and create irreparable damage to their psyches, Chico and I decided to drop the show altogether.

So here I was, doing occasional guest appearances, many of them on the Rudy Vallee Sealtest Show, biding my time, knowing that prosperity was just around the corner.

Then it happened. Success again. A radio variety show, sponsored by Pabst Beer, went on the air in March of 1943. My partners in crime were Virginia O'Brien, Donald Dickson, and Kenny Baker. The owners of the company were so pleased with my services that they adopted me into the family. I'm sure they meant well, but they made no effort to also adopt Harpo, Chico, Gummo, and Zeppo. So at the age of fifty-plus, I became the product of a broken home.

I didn't even look back. The honeymoon with the Pabsts would last forever.

It was February, 1944, and Pabst was celebrating its 100th Anniversary. I was to be the star of the festivities in Milwaukee. As soon as I arrived, I met a fine old gentleman named Edward Pabst, the scion of the family. He was almost eighty at the time, and a finer man never drew a soberer breath. Now I'd been taught to respect age, and it was very easy to respect dear Mr. Pabst. He was as alert and vital as yours truly, and I asked him to bend elbows with me.

Mr. Pabst, despite his illustrious family name, was not much of a drinker. In my conviviality, I kept urging more beer on him. The upchuck of the matter is that we both got quite tipsy, and an eager photographer captured for eternity that the beer I had been forcing down Mr. Pabst was Miller's High Life. The seedy picture-snapper wanted me to pay him off, which was a novelty, to say the least. This was the first time in my life someone had tried to blackmail me with pictures . . . and with my clothes on, yet.

You know what happened. No sooner did I return to California than the show was canceled, with no reason given. This would be straightened out quickly. I called Mr. Pabst to

12

see if he might intercede. The connection never got through. I became quite angry. If the phone service was this poor on a routine long distance call, then I apparently had my money in the wrong investment. I immediately sold all my stock in American Tel & Tel.

I could have buried my sorrows in drink, but that would have been playing into their hands. Besides, a truck had come up to the delivery entrance of the Marx Manor in Beverly Hills and taken away the same beer it had delivered gratis only the week before. If I was going to bury my sorrows, it wasn't going to be in *their* drink. It may have been the beer that made Milwaukee famous, but it succeeded in making me furious.

Anger turned to fever, which raged for days. My wife finally was able to make out what I was feebly saying, over and over. "Radio . . . radio."

I had mastered every other form of entertainment. Vaudeville, the Broadway stage, movies, Rotary smokers. Why should radio be such an elusive success? There had to be a way for me to master the medium.

All the while I was agonizing over my future, silent forces were at work putting together another radio show for me.

> *IRVING BRECHER: Gummo came to me and asked me to write a radio show for Groucho. I really didn't have anything in mind, because I was happy doing pictures. But Gummo was persistent. I told him, "The only thing I've got is something called* The Flotsam Family. *I read it to him and he asked, "Would you do it for Groucho?" Being a friend, I couldn't say no.*
>
> *It was a family comedy . . . the first comedy on radio where the father was amusing. The only other family comedy was where that idiot child, Henry Aldrich, cried, "Coming, Mother!" They auditioned the show, but it didn't sell.*

Everybody wants to get into the act. Brecher intrudes himself before I had a chance to give him an introduction. He is a screenwriter who wrote *At the Circus* and *Go West,* and whom I'd taken under my wing. A good friend.

So now seems as good a time as any to inform you that

13

throughout this epic narrative, friends and associates will interject their comments.

I read a lot, and one of the most irritating things about autobiographies is the way the first person describes himself in the most selfless way, more sinned against than sinning.

Everyone is going to have a chance to offer his viewpoint in this book. And though I may not agree with what they say, I might add parenthetically that I may not agree with what they say. Yet I am magnanimously offering them a forum. This is done after extensive conversations with the Federal Communications Commission. They keep repeating some rather fuzzy words: Equal Time.

You can't tell the program without the players, so allow me to introduce them at this time:

John Guedel: My partner on the show, who put the package together and who functioned as executive producer.

Robert Dwan: The director of *You Bet Your Life,* largely responsible for maintaining the taste level of the program.

Bernie Smith: Nominally the codirector, he was in effect the show's producer and supervised the program staff.

George Fenneman: Boy announcer.

Hy Freedman: The senior member of the program staff, and a top comedy writer.

Edwin I. Mills: Vice-president in charge of selecting contestants.

Morrie Ryskind: Collaborator with George S. Kaufman, also screenwriter of *A Night at the Opera,* and one of my oldest friends.

Jerry Fielding: Conductor of the *You Bet Your Life* orchestra, 1949 to 1953.

Jack Meakin: His successor, 1953 until the end of the show's run.

Marion Pollock: Vice-president in charge of questions for the quiz.

Melinda Marx Berti: Daughter.

Pedro Gonzalez Gonzalez: Our funniest contestant.

Howard Harris: Member of the program staff and writer of witty sayings.

Edgar Bergen: Fellow Comedian.

Phyllis Diller: Comedienne whose first national television appearance was on *You Bet Your Life.*

Now, where were we? I think we were talking about Irv Brecher's abortive attempts to sell a situation comedy. He scouted around, trying to sell the show in some other form, when he couldn't sell me as the star. Symbolic that our sunken ship should be called *Flotsam,* and I'm trying to maintain control by nc . calling the deserting Brecher a rat.

We continued talking, however, despite the fact that I was pariah in the eyes of prospective sponsors, just as Houdini's gums were pyorrhea in mine . . . but that's another story which has nothing to do with these words, secret or otherwise.

"I think the show would probably sell with a burly Irishman," Brecher told me.

"That's twelve centuries removed from what I am," I answered.

"I think I'll try and sell it with an Irishman," he resolved.

I lost my temper for a moment. "What a revolting development this is," I observed.

"Say, that's clever," he enthused. "Can I use that line?"

"Why not?" I answered. "You've used everything else."

Brecher became visibly upset. He thought I was angry.

IRVING BRECHER: Then I met William Bendix, and I asked Gummo, who was Groucho's agent, to try to get Bendix involved. Which he did. Gummo contacted the agent. Bendix liked the script. I changed the title to The Life of Riley, *changed a few lines, and auditioned it.*

I can't remember what Flotsam's profession was, but it wasn't what Riley's was . . . Riley was a riveter. Life of Riley *didn't sell until this fellow Frank Ferren found the record of the audition at the bottom of a heap of old records. He was looking for a show and if it weren't for his persistence,* Life of Riley *would never have been aired. And when he found the record, there was no information on it as to who even handled it, owned it, or anything.*

15

It took him days to track it down and to call the William Morris agency to tell them, "I'm going to buy your show." And they said, "What show?" That's how lucky they were. It was 1943, and the commissions that started then and went on through the show's run on radio and television must have been over two million dollars.

When we went on television, Bendix wasn't available. I took Jackie Gleason for twenty-six weeks. The day that Pabst canceled us, I was awarded the first Emmy for the show. They didn't think Gleason had any future as a comedian. But I think he has a better future than Pabst Blue Ribbon. He's certainly bigger.

Those years of the mid-1940's were largely spent entertaining the troops, again. I wasn't making much money. I was getting out in front of audiences and keeping my name alive. These were happy times. Then the war abruptly ended, and I was out of work again.

Someone, I truly believe, was trying to tell me something.

The year was 1947. The President had outlined to Congress a concept to be called the Truman Doctrine, which would give economic and military aid to nations threatened by Marxism. I categorically deny that *A Night in Casablanca,* my seventh farewell picture with Harpo and Chico, had anything to do with this new policy, though I must admit that I had difficulty in renewing mine. We were unable to get financing for our next film. It was to be the first disaster picture, *Shark Soup.*

But it wasn't to be. The project was canned. So were Harpo, Chico, and I.

It was about this time when all of Hollywood was accused of turning Marxist. You couldn't tell it by me. I didn't notice any more names on my dance program.

The town had come to a standstill. Anyone not working was automatically classified as a Commie, and I was beginning to get a little nervous until a bolt out of the blue, in the form of independent producer Sam Coslow, came knocking at my door.

Coslow wanted to star me in a musical, *Copacabana.* At last my singing talents were being recognized. He didn't want

16

Harpo and Chico, only me. That meant Harpo and Chico would not be working.

I went to work on the film in the spring of 1947, ten years after we, the Marx Brothers, had made our biggest hits at MGM.

I had a peachy time, but as shooting progressed I began to worry that after the picture was released the audience would give me the raspberry. For it soon became obvious that I was playing second banana to the tropical fruit on Carmen Miranda's head. And I found it difficult to submerge my star power to a papier-mâché kumquat. But the producer assured me that the audience was crazy about artificial fruit. Which was the start of Jack Lemmon's career.

I welcomed distraction from shooting, a guest appearance on a radio show with Bob Hope.

JOHN GUEDEL: There was a Walgreen show that had a lot of different stars who were all brought together for a two-hour special. It was a big radio show because it was a penny sale, which Walgreen put on once a year. This was before television and therefore it was their idea of a spectacular on the radio, you see. I was partners with Art Linkletter on People Are Funny, *and we were also doing* House Party. *We were doing a seven-minute section from* People Are Funny. *Art was supposed to interview a contestant while the contestant was bent over the lap of a pretty girl. The girl was blindfolded, and she was to take and sew the diaper on the contestant's pants. My job as the producer of* People Are Funny *was to hand the needle to Art. So you can see I had a big job that particular night.*

Bob Hope had a section of the show; Groucho had a section. So did Dinah Shore. We were all there for four or five hours, and I had this pipe box that intrigued Groucho. I didn't know him. I'd just met him. He said, "What do you carry in there?" I'd been carrying this for years, and I still carry everything in it, because you know a woman has a purse and a man should have his pipe box.

We did our bit, and I was sitting in the audience. Bob Hope was doing this routine with Groucho. He dropped his script while he was talking to Groucho . . . accidentally. Groucho dropped his on purpose because Bob Hope did, and as a result, they really tore the house down. They got a little dirty, but nevertheless it was on tape, you know.

17

Like the recollections of virtually everyone else in this lively tome, Guedel's are a bit off kilter. This is what actually happened on that historic day.

The time was April, 1947. Bob Hope was master of ceremonies for an all-star radio special. The spots were running longer than usual, and I had to cool my heels—and other nether regions—waiting to go on to do my two-spot with Hope midway through the program.

We were to do a sketch in which Hope was running a radio station in the middle of the Sahara, and I would be playing a traveling salesman. Since I'd played traveling salesman to many a farmer's daughter, it was type casting.

I came on to a deafening roar of applause. "Why, Groucho Marx!" Hope read. "What are you doing way out here in the Sahara Desert?"

"Desert, hell," I extemporized, "I've been standing in a drafty corridor for forty-five minutes."

This broke up the audience, as well as Hope, who in his hilarity dropped the script. I casually stepped on it.

"Hope, a pretty fair ad libber himself," my son Arthur wrote in *Life With Groucho,* "quickly entered into the spirit of the thing, and before Mannie Manheim or Charlie Isaacs (the show's writers and producers) could figure out how to stop them, the two comics had made an absolute shambles of their carefully prepared show. The spot ran twenty-five minutes over length, and much of it would never have passed the censors. Among a great many other off-color remarks, Groucho and Hope, all through the spot, had made frequent references to a notorious Los Angeles madam of a few years back."

After the show, Guedel sought me out. "Can you ad lib like that all the time?" he asked.

"Ask Sam Harris or George Kaufman," I answered breezily. "Or read any of those books that have legendary anecdotes about show business."

He looked at me in puzzlement, so I went on to explain.

18

"When I was doing *Cocoanuts* with my brothers, we were very fond of Kaufman, and tried to improve his script as much as we could. It was another of our typical long-runs, and the lines would have gotten stale anyhow. It was a thankless job, and Kaufman, by the way, never thanked us.

"One day Kaufman was standing backstage talking to Heywood Broun, while we were performing. All of a sudden he interrupted Broun in mid-sentence and walked over to the edge of the scrim. He came back a moment later. 'Why did you stop me in the middle of the story?' Broun asked. Kaufman replied, 'I had to. For a minute there I thought I heard one of the original lines of the play.' And you ask if I can ad lib all the time. I've ad libbed a whole Broadway show many a time."

In fact, Kaufman later told me I was the only actor he'd ever allow to ad lib his lines. That's why we got along together. Which reminds me of another story. I was once walking down a street with him in Boston. We passed by a jewelry store, Shreve, Crump & Low, which was like Tiffany's there. Kaufman turned to me and said, 'I wonder how those three fellows got together.' "

JOHN GUEDEL: Afterwards I went up to Groucho in the dressing room. I said, "Hiring you to do a show in which you read the script is like buying a Cadillac to haul coal. You're not getting all out of you that is desired. In other words, you're so much better ad libbing than talking to another stooge." I also said, "It gives you more reality. You might talk to real people for a change. A real old maid and a real truck driver and a real librarian rather than other people holding scripts, because your character comes over thin and brittle, just jokes and that's all, whereas I think you have a certain warmth."

So he said, "What do you have in mind?" I said, "I want you to do a quiz show." He answered, "I've flopped four times on radio before. I'm interested in anything. I might as well compete with refrigerators. I'll give it a try."

What Guedel didn't know was that I was pulling his leg. . . I'd been through that route before, and it had quickly become evident that my lightning wit and rakish charm overqualified me for what were passing as quizmasters in those days.

I neglected to tell him that I'd been approached to succeed Phil Baker on *The $64 Question*. Five others, unknown to me, also were sounded out. My audition record was sensational! But Eddie Cantor won out by a nose.

Once Guedel discovered the same thing, he would temper his enthusiasm. I fully expected not to hear from him again, and erased his memory from my mind. But he was just as eager to get started when he called me the following day.

Had I known about Guedel's shady past—though my experience with him up to now should have given me some clue—I might have given the enterprise greater thought.

To reveal his dark secret today actually can do little harm. He's made his millions, and *that* you can't take away from him. In fact, I've had trouble taking my millions away from him. But that's beside the point, and I don't want you the reader to lose interest. I've lost enough for both of us.

For what would the world have thought back then in 1947 if it had known that John Guedel invented the singing commercial?

This was in June of 1938. The Marx Brothers were at the peak of their form, making *Room Service* at RKO, which gave an unknown starlet named Lucille Ball a break.

Guedel was listening to the Jack Benny radio show. The Sportsmen Quartet, at the end of the commercial, sang "J . . . E . . . L . . . L . . . O."

A brainstorm struck Guedel. He would write an entire commercial in song. He hired four members of the Paul Taylor Chorus, then appearing on the Bing Crosby show, and wrote a series of singing commercials on speculation for the Ford Motor Company. They didn't sell.

This got his dander up. He resolved to show them. He took the same commercials, wrote new lyrics, and sold them to Birely's Orange Juice.

The rest is history. Next came the prestigious Butternut Bread account in Kansas City.

As Bernie Smith says, Guedel's contribution to social history puts him on a caste level a notch above Jack the Ripper's. And here I was, about to give his name legitimacy. I began to have fresh doubts.

IRVING BRECHER: I was on a fishing trip with Groucho and two friends, Frank Ferren and E. J. Rosenberg. Both were radio producers. Incidentally, Groucho wrote about this in his book, Groucho and Me, *but I don't think he saw it as funny as it was, because my memory on this is a little more accurate than what I saw in the book.*

The trip started when we three minus Groucho decided to go fishing, and thinking that he might enjoy it, I telephoned him. "Groucho, how would you like to go fishing in Wyoming?"

He said, "Are you crazy? I'm sitting here in a very expensive house, in a big Morris chair, with a Havana cigar, listening to my Capehart player. And do you think I'm going to leave all this to go fishing with some bums?" And he hung up the phone.

A half hour later he called and said, "My wife has my bag packed. When can you pick me up?" He was then married to Kay, Melinda's mother. I said, "We're going from here to Salt Lake City, and then to Wyoming." He said, "You can pick me up in Salt Lake City." I said, "I thought we were going together." He answered, "I wouldn't ride across the desert with fellows like you. It's too hot." At that time there was no air conditioning in cars. We agreed to meet in Salt Lake City. When we got together there by appointment, and on the way out of Salt Lake, Groucho said, "In case we die on the desert . . . rather, are threatened by death from thirst, I'd better get some tomatoes." So we stopped the car and he bought three tomatoes.

(I always have tomatoes with me when I think I'm going to die on the desert, and don't think I haven't been out with a number of them.)

He brought them out in a brown bag and all through the next ten days he kept offering us a tomato. Nobody would take them. Back in Beverly Hills ten days later, he had this bag of three rotten tomatoes. I don't know what he's done with them. He may still have them.

(I had them stewed when I got home.)

21

Groucho had never been fishing. We first got to Jackson Hole, then went on to Moran. We'd made arrangements with an unknown guide by telephone, a fellow by the name of Bob Robards, who was the cousin of Jason Robards, the actor. The moment Groucho saw him, he said, "This man looks like an embezzler. Let's go back." But we were too far away from home to do that. He remained suspicious of Robards, who was promising us that when we got to the campsite, there'd be sirloin steaks, all sorts of fine hors d'oeuvres, great bedding, and so on. He put us on pack mules, and we went through hot springs that bubbled out of the earth. There were deerflies as big as dachshunds attacking us. It was incredible. By the time we got to this lousy camp, we were exhausted. Groucho was getting sick, and he was furious with us. We were really at the point past the hysterical laugh. It was just grim. This great campsite that Robards promised us was a tent with some shredded canvas on one side of it. And we realized, as Robards reluctantly confirmed, that a bear had torn it. The night before, Robert Taylor, the actor, whom we knew, had been in there fishing, had used the tent, and had flown out on an aquaplane. So we had the tent, and we had Spam for dinner. Nobody could eat it.

(Even the mosquitoes wouldn't eat it.)

The mosquitoes were just awful, so we'd rub ourselves with citronella, and got nauseous from the smell.

During the night Groucho said, "I want you to bury me near the lake." He was that sick. I was worried, because I was very young at the time and he was, naturally, older. You know, he was an elderly man. Anytime a man is a few years older, you think of him as an elderly man.

After he recovered that morning, we forced some coffee into him, and he seemed to be a little better. He finally said, "Where's the men's room?" Robards said, "You use the woods, Groucho."

(Robards got a big laugh out of this. I was to use the woods, he informed me, "the same as everybody else.")

So Groucho disappeared in the woods. A few minutes later he came running back with his pants down, crouched, and he said, "Don't look now, but there's a bear following me." We ran out and looked, and in the thicket there was a bear cub—brown bear—no threat. Someone asked him what had happened. He said, "Well, I was sitting there waiting for nature to take its course. I looked up and I saw a hand waving at me from the bushes. I waved back, and then I realized that the hand had claws on it. So I decided that it might not be a member of

22

our party, and I decided to get out. And this goddamn bear came after me." Groucho threatened to sue me, Ferren, and Rosenberg for attempted murder. I got movies of the bear. It was hilarious.

Coming back from the trip, we were talking about radio. I owned Life of Riley, *and I was really deep into radio. I was also writing films. Groucho was trying to feel out our opinions, because the other men were experts in the field. I was the closest one to him personally. When he said, "I have no intention of doing a quiz show," I didn't want to say to him, "You're wrong." I figured I'd better stay out of this. I also doubted, having written two pictures for him, and having such great respect for his talent, whether he could stand up there every week and deal with the peasants. But Ferren particularly, and Rosenberg too, both sensed he could be great doing this. Happily, he changed his mind. And they were right.*

All right. Let's get the show on the road. During our discussions, Guedel would jot down all sorts of figures, showing how much money we would make on capital gains and debentures and stock options. It looked all right to me. I've always had a trusting nature, and I couldn't make out the figures anyway.

It was a motley crew that Guedel brought over from Art Linkletter's *House Party.* But it might have been motlier if Linkletter had come along. This crew had made significant contributions to Linkletter's stock portfolio, which was bulging even then.

And how had they contributed to these many millions? Simply by devising all sorts of cute tricks for Art to play on the long-suffering audience. He would encourage the children on his show to air their family's dirty linen. Then he'd shake his head and say, "Kids say the darndest things."

He would also riffle through the purses of women in the audience, and what he found in them was unmentionable in high-class company.

Linkletter had made millions. This was the route Groucho would also take. I would entrust my life and future to a bunch of voyeurs.

Newsweek, in describing my capitulation, said it was like

selling Citation to a glue factory. I don't know why they said that. I'd never even gotten a parking ticket.

BERNIE SMITH: John Guedel was a game-show man, instinctively. We got to thinking about a format, a game show where Groucho could ad lib with the contestants. He never really thought it was going to be that much ad lib, though. John thought it was going to be mainly a quiz show with fun and games.

We went out to Groucho's. I'd never met him before. John said, "Bernie, I want you to meet Groucho Marx." I said, "This is a great pleasure." Groucho, I'll never forget, was sitting in a window seat. I'm sure in the back of his mind he's thinking, here's the great Groucho about to do a lousy quiz show. He didn't look at me. "It's no great pleasure," Groucho said. "I've known him for years."

Anyway, here he was placing his whole career in my hands, and he'd never heard of me. John told him I'd been on People Are Funny, *that he'd known me a long time, and that I was a very talented guy.*

Groucho asked, "How much are we paying him?"

"Three hundred a week," John said.

And Groucho said, "He can't be any good. You can't get a good writer for less than nine hundred a week."

There was a very simple solution. John called me in. "You're fired," he told me. "And now you're rehired at nine hundred." He went back to Groucho and said, "I've got a nine-hundred-a-week writer." That was the end of that. Groucho didn't question it.

We proceeded to put the show together. Guedel and his staff would come up with some ideas. I rejected them all.

"What is it exactly that you want?" Guedel asked wearily, thinking I was being obstinate.

I had some definite ideas about the show, but no one bothered to consult me. At last, here was Guedel waiting to hear them.

"I want gaiety, laughter, ha-cha-cha."

Guedel gulped, audibly. "I'm sorry. No ha-cha-cha. This is a family show."

Getting two out of my three demands wasn't bad, so I didn't press the point. There were other problems to be overcome.

24

I wasn't particularly proud of doing a quiz show. It was like slumming. I told Harpo, who tooted his horn sympathetically. The solution was obvious, and it had taken Harpo's simple, loving wisdom to point it out.

I would simply have to take charge and toot my own horn. I would lay down the law to these rank amateurs.

I had my standards, and I knew what I would and would not do. I let these cohorts know right away that I would not do an insult number on the contestants, then try to win them back at the end of the sequence with some schmaltz. I had too much pride to do that, and if that's what they wanted, they'd better get another star.

There was another matter to iron out before we proceeded.

"In eight years, the whole quiz show concept will be altered by *The $64,000 Question*," Guedel told me. "Why don't we steal their thunder and give huge cash prizes now?"

"Because," I patiently told him, "the show's budget is only five thousand dollars a week."

He nodded slowly, then continued chewing his gum.

"Besides," I continued, "money will never make you happy and happy will never make you money. That might be a wisecrack, but I doubt it."

> *JOHN GUEDEL: I think the best symbols or the best things that catch on are done more or less casually and accidentally, and only by looking backwards do they become important. I was just looking desperately for something to put at the end of the show. I said, "Well, we always can use a big wheel." A lot of people thought that was very good. It's a stupid old idea. I mean, there's been big wheels for years in the carnies and now you look at all these daytime shows on television and they've all got this stuff going around. It's very big money now.*

Guedel and I had some big money going on the project ourselves. We'd become partners and each put up $125 for an audition record. We decided we would cut it before an audience of Linkletter's *House Party*. We had some further last-minute refinements to work out.

The discussion group included Bob Dwan, who was writing *People Are Funny* and working at NBC as staff director, and who had been hired as director of our show; Bernie Smith, the codirector, who would also head the program staff and eventually function as the show's unofficial producer; Eddie Mills, the "people getter" and, naturally, Guedel with his ubiquitous pipe box.

BERNIE SMITH: The greatest entrance cue in the history of the theater, that made a big impression on me, was in Marc Connelly's Green Pastures. *In the first act, where the Lord is ready to make his entrance, the Archangel Gabriel gets everybody's attention, and at the top of his voice, he says, "Make way for the Lord God Jehovah!" You can't beat it.*

I put Groucho in the same class. I wanted to bring him on in the same way. So in the first script that I wrote, I had the announcer saying, "Now, here he is, the funniest man in the world, Groucho Marx!" Which is a pretty strong line. Well, I took it to Groucho, who had to approve it. He said, "I'm not the funniest man in the world. And even if I were, when you say something like that, I'd better be pretty funny." I saw his point. I thought about it some more. I still wanted to bring him on with a blast of bugles. That's where I came up with the idea of having the audience bring him on. If one announcer is good, let's have two hundred and fifty announcers. I wanted something unique. I wanted to put the audience into the show right away, and I wanted to bring Groucho on with a big blast. So that's what we used on the first show, and we kept it right on through.

ROBERT DWAN: The big decision Groucho made was to come on in his own character without the black mustache. Without the frizzy hair. Playing himself and not a clown was a major change in his whole approach. Now he established a whole new Groucho character. It was partly based on Dr. Hackenbush and the others but this was not the same guy at all, and it allowed him to do things and to react in other ways.

BERNIE SMITH: In all the success that Groucho had, in movies, on Broadway, on radio, the public never knew what he looked like. The only time the public saw him was when he had the fake mustache and the frock coat and his hair was all frizzed. So he could walk around in plain clothes and nobody knew who he was. For an actor who has a built-in ego this would kind of hurt.

When we went on radio I said, "Groucho, you have to wear your frock coat and the fake mustache." He said, "The hell I will. That character's dead. I'll never go into that again." And I answered, "Well, the public won't know who you are. We've got to have you in something." But he wouldn't do it.

I asked, "Well, will you grow a mustache? A real mustache?" He said, "That I'll do." And that's why he has the mustache today, because we talked him into it.

JOHN GUEDEL: In 1947 we were running a thing on People Are Funny *where if an alarm clock went off any time while the person was talking, they'd get some money or something like that. And any idea which would have an over-enveloping umbrella that could start at the first of the program and continue to the end always intrigued me. We didn't have anything to tie this show together, because it was just three separate quizzes. I wanted to have something that, whatever it was, was going to happen instantly. So instead of using the alarm clock, we used a secret word. This worked out a lot better. You can fix an alarm clock, you know, to go off almost any time you want. Actually, it was a substitute for the alarm clock. The secret word was just a thing to throw in at the last minute on the audition.*

Consequently, with *House Party* announcer Jack Slattery in tow, I cut the record.

For the purposes of this book, I'm happy that Bernie Smith saves everything.

For he possesses the last existing record of that audition. I listened to it the other day, and I don't say I was nervous, but my delivery was so staccato and rapid-fire that I sound like one of those bad imitations of yours truly.

The only thing memorable about that show, as I see it, was a question I asked the young couple who were the first contestants. For the sake of trivia fans, they should be identified as "Just Mets" (interested in getting married) named Myrtle

27

McKuen and Robert Brooks. Miss McKuen was a twenty-two-year-old waitress; Brooks, at twenty-four, was a clothes salesman. ("Just Mets," by the way, was the phrase Bernie Smith conjured up to describe our matchmaking efforts on the show. You know the story: Boy Meets Girl . . . Romeo and Juliet . . . Minneapolis and St. Paul).

The question I asked the two was this: "Is it proper to break a piece of bread or roll in the soup?"

They answered, correctly, "No."

"It's very improper," I agreed, "especially to roll in the soup."

If Guedel couldn't sell the show on the strength of that profundity, then I'd better get another partner.

JOHN GUEDEL: I took it to all three networks, and all three turned it down. And so you can't sell it to networks. I couldn't sell People Are Funny to the networks either. I sold it to clients. That's a big difference.

It was only the fifth week after we made the record. I read a gossip column in Daily Variety which said that Al Gellman, the president of Elgin-American Compact Company, was coming to the Beverly Hills Hotel to sign Phil Baker for his new quiz show, Everybody Wins. The item said, "coming to," that means he hadn't signed him yet. So I called him up at the hotel and told him, "I have a record of Groucho." Gellman said, "Groucho Marx. I remember him in The Cocoanuts." I played the record for him, and he thought it was pretty good. He didn't know Groucho flopped four times on the radio, so he bought the show for Elgin-American Compacts. Then we took it to the American Broadcasting Company, and that's how it happened to be on ABC.

Phil Baker, I understand, fired his press agent for putting that item in the gossip column before the deal was actually signed. I don't blame him.

The sponsor had a couple of suggestions before agreeing to put us on the air. Suggestions in this case meant demands.

Although he respected Jack Slattery's talents, he wanted a fresh voice to do the commercial spiels for the product. Slattery was too identified with the Linkletter stable, and he would prove to be the first casualty of the show. He would act as my assistant on the first couple of shows, introducing the contestants and so forth, with the commercials to be read by a new announcer. This second fellow would assume all the duties within a short time.

GEORGE FENNEMAN: Bob Dwan hired me, but indirectly. I ran into him at the corner of Hollywood and Vine. Bob was my boss in San Francisco at the American Broadcasting Company up there. He was program director. I'd transferred to ABC in Los Angeles. He didn't even know I was in town. It was on my lunch hour. And he said, "George!" "Bob!" He said, "Come with me. They're doing an audition for a new nutty show with Groucho Marx. We don't know what's going to happen to it, but they're auditioning for commercial announcers." I said, "I can't. I have a station break." He said, "Make a phone call and come." So I did and there were like thirty-five announcers in this recording studio. I recorded my audition . . . this was just a bunch of people in the basement. And then I won it. Still I hadn't met Groucho. Then the next week I was doing the show up on the stage with my hero from my high school days. When I was a kid the Marx Brothers pictures were a big event. And you know, that's the amazing thing . . . the longevity. The fact that this man has had a career in every medium, and a big one. And to suddenly be on the stage with him was overpowering.

I understand perfectly. I get that same feeling whenever I have to appear on stage myself. I may have been more nervous than usual as we made last minute preparations for the first show, which was to be aired on ABC on October 27, 1947.

ROBERT DWAN: We were supposed to be on live, but the day before we were supposed to go on radio, somebody got nervous and we decided to record it. We did it on big acetate disks that could be edited. Once that was decided, there was no reason why Groucho couldn't record for as long as we wanted. At that time the only people using them were Armed Forces Radio. It was developed by them to take commercials out of shows for broadcast overseas, and I was the only one who did it commercially.

29

We recorded in ten-minute segments. A guy would set up three of these big thirty-three-and-a-third platters on three turntables like a sound effects playback.

The edits were always on laughs. We would fade one laugh into the other. We did this the whole first season at ABC.

Then a fellow named Mullen liberated a machine called an Ampex from Germany during the war and brought it here. Myrdo McKenzie, Bing Crosby's director, had one set, and I had the other. We did the first editing of audio tape for the Crosby show and You Bet Your Life.

And so we were off and running.

In later years, a great controversy was to break out. People were dying to find out whether my show was actually as ad lib as the network and sponsors claimed. I suppose an answer from me is expected. Well I'm going to answer with a question. Wouldn't you like to know?

JOHN GUEDEL: We didn't want to call anyone a writer, for this was an ad lib show. So Bernie Smith, who was the head of the writing, was called a director. The other writers were put on the program staff.

A great deal of the show was ad libbed. The Groucho show was similar to building a wall. The scaffolding is the written material. Then you put up the wall, and then often you tear down the scaffolding. So you take out the written material and leave in the ad libs because they seem to come out more spontaneously, obviously. That's the end result: you need scaffolding to build a wall.

I cannot go any further without saying that Bernie Smith, Ed "Doc" Tyler, Hy Freedman, and Howard Harris wrote some of the sweetest ad libs a comedian ever spoke. It would then be up to me to scatter the buckshot.

At the outset, the show was scripted. It went like this:

MONDAY, OCTOBER 27, 1947   ABC   5:00 to 5:30 P.M.

SLAT (quiet dignity)

Ladies and Gentlemen. At any moment during the next half-hour, someone might receive one thousand dollars in cash . . . *at any moment.*

GROUCHO

Really?

SLAT

YOU BET YOUR LIFE!
MUSIC: (Theme . . . Up and Under)

SLAT

Elgin-American, creators of America's most beautiful compacts—smartest cigarette cases—finest dresser sets—presents Groucho Marx in *You Bet Your Life,* the show that has the thousand-dollar bell that rings at the mention of the mystery word. And here's the star of our show, a man to whom we all pay tribute . . .

GROUCHO

My landlord?

SLAT

One whose loyal *fans* are everywhere . . .

GROUCHO

Sally Rand?

SLAT

The one, the only . . .

AUDIENCE

GROUCHO!

GROUCHO

That's *me* . . . Groucho Marx!
MUSIC: (Theme . . . Up and Finish Over Applause)
   (APPLAUSE)

GROUCHO

Thank you. Well, this is what I get for coming in too late to get a seat. . . . Folks, this is just as new to me as it is to you. I've never done one of these shows before. I only came in tonight because I heard they were giving away one thousand dollars in cash. Now I find out I'm the one who gives it away. Jack Slattery, who's first to play *You Bet Your Life?*

SLAT

All our couples drew straws for positions in the race for the thousand dollars. And here's the couple that drew the shortest straw . . . Miss . . . . and Mr. . . . . , meet the man with all the money, Groucho Marx!

GROUCHO

Welcome to *You Bet Your Life*. Folks, we advertised for a lot of people to come to the show tonight who are interested in getting married, but who haven't found the right mate yet. And just before we went on the air, these two volunteers were chosen from the audience. Have you two ever seen each other before?

(No)

Never been properly introduced?

(No)

Miss . . . . , shake hands with Mr. . . . .

(They greet each other)

I now pronounce you man and wife. Next contestants, please.

SLAT

Groucho! You're going too fast!

GROUCHO

Well, I guess I was a little hasty. Miss . . . . . . , have you looked at your compact lately? Other people do, you know! And here's a gift you'll want to look at and admire often, and other people will too . . . an Elgin-American *playtime* compact. What do you think of *that?*

(She says)

And, Mr. . . . . . . , here's your gift from Elgin-American, a sterling silver cigarette case. Isn't it a beauty?

(He says)

Well, so you both want to get married, eh?

(Yes)

After interview:

GROUCHO

Well, for a couple that's just met for the first time, you two are getting along fine. Now let's see how you can work together when the chips are down. You're going to have a chance to win up to one thousand four hundred and eighty dollars . . . by working together as a team. *You Bet Your Life!*

SLAT

Each couple on stage has been credited with twenty dollars

on our books. Groucho will ask each couple three questions.

And you bet me you can answer those questions . . . bet as much of your twenty dollars as you want to. The couple earning the most money by the end of the show gets a chance at a thousand-dollar question. How'd you like a chance at the thousand bucks right this minute?

(They say)

Well, if you mention a certain *secret word* anytime you're up here talking, a bell will ring like this:

SOUND: FIRE ALARM

When the bell rings, I'll ask you the thousand-dollar question immediately, and if you answer it right, you collect the thousand.

(Groucho, go right into top of next page)

FADE DOWN:

SLAT

This is Jack Slattery offstage (where no one in the studio can hear me). The secret word is . . . . . . If anybody says the word . . . . . . he gets a chance at the thousand-dollar question immediately. Now back to Groucho.

GROUCHO

The secret word is a common, everyday word used all the time. Here's a hint: You can't say a thing without using it. Ohhhh! I practically told you! The word is on the other side of that cardboard, so you see we can't fool you. I wonder which of our couples is going to win the most money? Remember, the more you bet, the more you *win!* Okay, here's your first question: It's on food. For example, if I asked: "What is raised in wet, tropical countries," the answer would be "umbrellas!" That wouldn't be right, but you'd get a laugh. Now how much of your twenty bucks are you going to bet you can answer your first question? It pays even money. Bet ten, make ten. Go ahead, talk it over between yourselves. Take all the time you want . . . I'll give you *five seconds.*

After the three sets of contestants answered the questions, the plan was for me to go down into the audience to engage in some sort of interplay. Listeners would send in problems to be answered, and members of the audience would try their hands at being Dear Abbys.

Then we would come back to the winning couple, standing in front of the microphone, ready to answer the jackpot question. If they answered it, I would then blurt out:

GROUCHO

You're both Elgin-Americans; the best there are! Yes, sir, you came through with *flying colors* . . . you're both *pale-green!*

If anyone can surmount that material, he's entitled to success.

The show zoomed to ninety-second in the ratings. Being ninety-second wasn't too red-hot, but it wasn't bad for ABC, which wasn't called the third network for nothing, for I think it only had three stations. We had the figures where they counted, however, for sales of Elgin-American compacts rose spectacularly.

> *JOHN GUEDEL: Gellman wanted to know if he could just run up until Christmas and then stop, because that's when ninety-five percent of his business was, and then kind of hang on the rest of the year. I guess if the show hadn't been a big success you might go along with a thing like that, but we'd stretch him a few weeks beyond Christmas, and then make him run some repeats. And Gellman didn't like me because I carried my pipe box. He told Gummo, "Anybody that carries a pipe box is suspicious." But he was getting good sales and a good audience right from the start.*

Now anyone can tell by Guedel's foregoing comments that storm clouds might be brewing. Not my crew. They were so happy to be getting regular paychecks that they thought it would last forever. I knew otherwise. To stay on top requires work.

The audience was already giving us signals on how to proceed. Part of the quiz always had a funny twist to the ques-

34

tion. As an example, the question on the audition record, "Is it proper to break a piece of bread or roll in the soup?" We quickly found out from the audience that they wanted the quiz section to be seriously conducted. The contestants might be flying through hoops only moments before, but when we turned to the quiz, no matter how little money was at stake, we had to mean business.

HY FREEDMAN: I was hired only to write jokes for the quiz. Of course, it was the wrong way around. I remember doing jokes for weeks on the quiz. But it was stopped because of the audience reaction against it. When we started out, Bernie Smith was the head writer, and I was on the writing staff. We soon added a second writer, Elroy Schwartz.

Maybe I had a Groucho viewpoint, and that's why I fit in. One of the things that is distinctive in his delivery is that it's difficult to tell when he's reading or when he's ad libbing his own line. It's picking at things, it's needling things, it's confusing things, it's the pun, the setting them up for the joke.

You're getting it in all the dimensions. If you just set it down on paper, the line is nothing. The only thing that works are good jokes, and well-constructed jokes. Good sharp lines. But if they'd been real sharp, carefully constructed jokes, I don't think the program would have worked. How could a man stand up there and come up with gem after gem? Sometimes he wouldn't even have to say a line. A pretty girl would come out and up would go the eyebrows. It was a great show for a writer, an easy and pleasurable show to do.

There was another area where I felt my spontaneity was being tampered with. Guedel had devised a system where I would meet with contestants before we went on the air.

This lasted for the first three weeks of the show. It just wasn't effective. The program staff might have a pretty good idea about what the contestants were going to say, and I might have a rough idea of my own words, but bringing us together for the first time on the air was that unpredictable factor that made the show a hit.

And it could be done with little preparation on my part. They say Milton Berle has a file of jokes as high as the Empire State Building. I didn't need such canned material. Everybody says something that lends itself to humor. People *are* funny.

EDWIN I. MILLS: One change that came very quickly was the practice of Groucho going down into the audience to talk to people as part of the warm-up. He hated doing it, and so we dropped it.

We would have these long warm-ups that sometimes were funnier than the shows themselves. Harpo and Chico would come on and horse around with Groucho. But they wouldn't appear on the show itself.

Finally Groucho said, "Let's not leave all our fun in the dressing room." We were doing too much.

Some of our early meetings were at Groucho's house, but most of the initial planning meetings were held in the office. Groucho rarely showed up for them.

Everyone was feeling his way. Refinements came by trial and error.

The contestants at first were picked from the audience. We'd invite several people with similar occupations and interview them before the show, with the audience selecting the contestants. We found this was leaving a lot to chance, and it wasn't giving Groucho a fair break.

Over the years we evolved to where we'd go for the personality. We began to invite guests. Groucho loved sports figures. Occasionally we'd recruit people from show business. Groucho also loved to debunk politicians, so we had quite a few of them on too.

At the beginning I'd go out and search for personalities. Later in the show's run, we might put in an ad in a Long Beach paper inviting people to come down to the De Soto showroom to be interviewed. Hundreds of people would show up, and I'd make pertinent notes about each one. After a while people would begin to call me about contestants.

We got to know what would work on the show. First, the contestant had to be an extrovert, a talker, who would volunteer things. These were people who were at ease and articulate, and who liked life. Groucho's main premise was to take a line and misconstrue it. We also discovered the audience didn't like people who were capable of landing on their feet. The clever, self-sufficient person with the snappy comeback didn't play well. It was more effective to have the contestants bumble their way into topping Groucho.

When the show first started to click, it seemed to spawn a lot of imitations with other comedians as stars. But none of them was as success-

ful. They all tried to find out how we did it. And yet, the concepts were basically simple.

I quickly developed an instinct to ferret out charlatans. We'd still get our share of duds. With amateurs there's no assurance of a performance. We'd have high hopes for them, and then the veil would pass over their faces.

We had great ethnic contestants . . . Italians, Yugoslavs. They talked about very basic things and in very simple terms. They seemed less inhibited. They were warm and marvelous. Eventually, we must have had every nationality on. The big quiz shows would call us and ask for people.

There were still more changes in the offing. I've never liked the sound of sirens, and I didn't like one blowing in my ear whenever someone said the secret word. We had to change that.

BERNIE SMITH: The duck was Groucho's idea. He said, "We ought to have something come down. An elephant or a pretty girl or a duck or something." I immediately said, "A duck is a funny animal. We'll use a duck."

When I told my brother Chico about the duck, he asked me, for the thousandth time, it seems, "Why a duck? Why a no-chicken?"

Believe me, you have to get up early around Chico if you want to get out of bed.

I fixed him with a steady stare. "Because."

Of course, then he understood.

BERNIE SMITH: Grant's Tomb was also his idea. Early in the game he said, "Gee, when people go broke up there I'm embarrassed. I feel they ought to have something, to give the thing an up note when they leave. Can't we ask a simple question, like, 'Who's the President of the United States?' or 'Who's buried in Grant's Tomb?' or something?" Grant's Tomb immediately clicked.

There were the rules for the quiz. They had to be clearly spelled out.

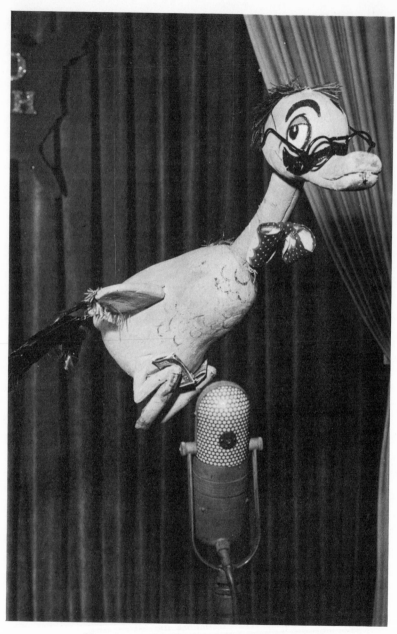

Here's one bird who never laid an egg.

If you analyze it, the rules of the game were quite simple: Each pair of contestants was given twenty dollars. They could bet any of that amount on the first question, and as the amount increased on the three following questions so that the couple winning the highest amount would be eligible for the $2,000 grand prize question, not to mention the $100 they may have already won on the secret word, which if added to the four questions they could consecutively answer without missing two in a row, would give them $1,000 and make them eligible to spin the wheel, depending on if they picked the respective numbers previously selected by the contestants for the $5,000 and $10,000 questions, or they could bet on the basic amount by answering questions naturally paying off more, say $300 to the $100 payoff on the question even your Aunt Gladys could answer; however, if George Fenneman was recruited to help answer the questions, they were allowed to pick two questions from Column A and one from Column B, because after all George was born in China, and this added a novel slant to the game, not to mention the fortune cookies, none of which contained the right answers, because we were a rigidly honest show and no help from the audience was permitted. This was why our show was so distinctive.

> *ROBERT DWAN: We always had a reason for the change in format. We were trying to make it better, trying to increase the suspense. We were trying to make the competition fair and even, but we always had to have something so that each set of contestants could be completed in a unit. There was no necessary connection between them, you know.*

Now we had hit our stride. We were beginning to mesh into a successful operation. Before long, we were even able to raise Fenneman's salary from its original $55 a week.

Elsewhere, the formula was still evolving.

> *BERNIE SMITH: We used to have a program meeting once a week with Ed Mills, Marion Pollock, and later Rich Hall. They would*

sit there with their stacks of notes and take turns submitting people to me. I had to have a gut reaction about contestants. If I could sense that they were really enthused about somebody, and I could see that the information was there and that they would be productive, then I would say, "Let's take them." I missed lots of times; it wasn't one hundred percent, but overall I think the average is pretty good.

There were times when the people might have to come back for three weeks. The staff might be trying to sell somebody to me, and there'd be something about them I didn't like. Finally, I'd say, "Okay, if you're that sold, we'll take him." And the contestant would turn out to be great, and was due to the persistence of the staff.

After I'd get the people I would assign them to various writers whenever they'd come in for interviews. I learned the knack of interviewing when I was a reporter for Hearst and Scripps-Howard. I translated that into what we did with the contestants.

There was no formula as such, other than just the training that you acquire. You learn how to do it, to find out what's productive, and you have an instinct, if you develop it.

There was still another thorn in my claw: how to draw Fenneman out.

"And now, here he is, the one, the only . . ."

GEORGE FENNEMAN: I wasn't hired to talk to Groucho, and I was a little afraid of him, of course. In the beginning I just did three commercials . . . the opening and the closing. I don't know how they introduced the characters—the contestants—but I don't think I did that in the beginning. Then he . . . I don't know . . . I either made a mistake on a commercial or, in some way, he drew me into it. And we started this byplay in front of the audience. Maybe he wouldn't let me finish the commercial. It started very innocently with no malice of forethought. Then I started doing all of it. When I started doing the arithmetic on the quizzes, it blossomed into this give-and-take, with me always on the receiving end. In the beginning I guess I took some of the humor personally. I know I wasn't stupid, but when I finished the show I wasn't sure.

Fenneman. Now there's a name to conjure up all sorts of visual pictures. The most obvious to me, of course, was Feenamint, and that's what I began to call him backstage.

I used to call Margaret Dumont Mrs. Rittenhouse after the hotel we stayed in when we played Philadelphia. Rittenhouse . . . Feenamint . . . to me they both meant the same thing.

"Feeling sluggish and out of sorts? Take Rittenhouse once a week to be sure."

I took Fenneman once a week too, to be sure, and I felt marvelous. He soon became my Mrs. Dumont, and I valued his contributions greatly. For there was never a comedian who was any good unless he had a good straight man. And George was straight on all four sides.

GEORGE FENNEMAN: And would you believe that my mother looked just like Margaret Dumont? She didn't have that distracted vagueness about her, since she was a Nevada ranch pioneer. But my mother was in many ways very naïve.

Mrs. Dumont never understood any of my jokes. George did. He was very bright, but he still made a good foil.

Of course, the name Fenneman, as a result, will live on forever. Why just the other day I got a letter from a fan: "I'm 5' 8½", brown hair, green eyes, light complexion and I'm

41

17½ and I have a lot of old-fashioned ways and I'm fun to be with and I love the smell of cigars."

Wrong letter. Here it is:

"By the way, we have a new insult around the school I go to. We call somebody Fenneman and then there is no comeback."

That's what I did for Fenneman. All right then. I'll concede that George himself had a lot to do with it.

JOHN GUEDEL: I used to tell Groucho, "You know, bring your daughter out to warm up the audience. Get them to like you." Melinda was a tiny little girl at the time. I told him to talk about her, and the audience would like him for that.

Sometimes he'd come off the show and say, "Wasn't I warm tonight? Wasn't I the Jewish Dr. Christian?"

Coincidentally, sometimes he'd go on the street, and a woman would come up to him, and he'd say, "Get lost." And she'd think it was so funny, and here he's really telling her to get lost. Anybody else they'd slap in the face.

IRVING BRECHER: I think Groucho's image was changed quite a bit on the show. He'd always been the raffish anti-Establishment destroyer. Now he was a more sedate man, dressed in a business suit with his hair neatly combed, holding a cigar, peering over his glasses, asking questions and making comments that were funny. These were two different images, but the vestiges of the first, from film and stage, were still there . . . the great delivery, the raised eyebrows. But there wasn't too much business on the show. He wasn't made up, he didn't have a false mustache. The other fellow is J. Cheever Loophole from At the Circus, a character from another planet. That motion picture image wouldn't have been as successful. If he'd gone up there with a crepe mustache, I don't think the show would have made it, because he would then be a heavy.

I don't know what Guedel and Brecher are talking about. Image simply means the picture that comes over the tube.

But speaking of heavy, as Brecher was a moment ago, more letters started flowing in. The audience didn't care if I stepped on the contestants, but they didn't want me talking rudely to Fenneman. To my great surprise, I discovered that some people disliked me because of the way I treated him. George was like a son to me. The give-and-take chemistry which evolved was part of my plan to help the kid. He was painfully shy. For all my efforts I became the near-villain.

GEORGE FENNEMAN: I was often at a loss for words. But I began to learn from Groucho that I could get a laugh from a facial reaction as well as from a witty line. I can't give any specifics, but I know that Groucho shocked me a lot of times. Very often I would be standing backstage and I'd hear him say, "Fenneman, come out here." I knew I was in trouble of some kind. Or Groucho would try to match me with somebody on the show. It was a good gimmick to embarrass George, and I think most people knew I was married happily to the same lady all those years and with three kids. And then of course if he did match me up, it would always be with a woman who liked to kiss and everything, you know. Then he would confess to her that I had three children. It was very funny, but my discomfiture was genuine.

I don't want to reflect badly on Fenneman, he's a sensitive boy, but have you ever seen anyone run on like he does? I think it all goes back to his start in radio, when he had to navigate the labyrinths which follow that immortal phrase, "And now a word from our sponsor."

BERNIE SMITH: I was the West Coast producer for We, the People, *which was a big radio show in New York. It wasn't broadcast out here. It was sponsored by Gulf Oil and it was on for years. They would find people, mostly stars, which was why I was doing it here, that they wanted interviewed. Then I'd go interview the people, then write it for a local emcee, who would carry on. Well, they gave me the names of Mr. and Mrs. Story.*

This had to be twenty-nine years ago, the first year of the show. My wife and I drove one Sunday to Bakersfield. Mr. Story was lying in a hammock under a fig tree. He'd been a sign painter, but he'd given up. He had twenty-two kids and that was too much for him. It was the largest family in the United States with the same mother and father. There were nineteen still living. Mrs. Story was built like a big baby machine. She was a big, stocky peasant type with legs that big around.

My wife and I had a little chat with them. Then it was lunchtime.

43

Mrs. Story brought a platter of sandwiches out to the front porch, where they ate, which was half as round as the table and stacked almost a foot high.

She said, "Come and get it." They came out of trees; they came out of windows. Pretty soon there's nineteen kids, all healthy, all bright. They had their own orchestra in the family. They did everything as a family unit. They weren't interested in other people.

I'm pretty sure we sent a bus up there to bring them all down so we could parade them across the stage.

Wherever I go, people ask me about a remark I purportedly made to Mrs. Story. Folklore about the encounter has been so broadly disseminated that it has been variously described as occurring with a mother having any number from ten to thirty children. The story, however, is not apocryphal. It did happen.

"Why do you have so many children?" I asked Mrs. Story. "That's a big responsibility and a big burden."

"Well," she replied, "because I love children, and I think that's our purpose here on earth, and I love my husband."

"I love my cigar too," I shot back, "but I take it out of my mouth once in a while."

That kind of remark can have one of two reactions. It will either cause a sharp intake of breath at having crossed some forbidden frontier or it will bring the house down. The studio audience loved it, but the people out there in Radioland never got a chance to react. The exchange was clipped out by Dwan, the house censor.

ROBERT DWAN: The suspicion that the show was basically censorable was much more real than the actuality. I didn't cut out very many things for reason of dirty material. I principally edited to get the cream out of the funny stuff. I think this takes a longer explanation. My training goes back to radio where you really had the star system working. Your whole objective in creating a show was to create an environment in which the star personality could operate. I think we did that to the ultimate degree with Groucho, because this whole vehicle was constructed to allow him to do his thing, what he could do the best,

44

the most comfortably. The whole structure of the show was designed to let him, in conversation with these people, know that they had something to talk about, but also to allow him to go on with any kind of tangent. He didn't feel that he had to have a joke every thirty seconds, which is what you would have had to do if the program were done, as many radio programs were, live direct broadcast.

Sooner than I expected, the show began to take shape and the crew meshed into a smooth and professional operation. We were getting to know and like one another as we went along.

> *BERNIE SMITH: Groucho and I were at the Beverly Hills Brown Derby having lunch one day. We'd just started the show and I didn't know him too well. I'm a quiet sort of a guy; I'm not an extrovert by a long ways. Groucho too had always been quiet. The place was jammed. If you remember, the Beverly Brown Derby has booths about waist high, with a flat surface on the top of the divider, which serpentines around the room. So he climbed on top of the booth and walked the whole length of the restaurant on that flat surface. I was so embarrassed, I wanted to dig a hole and crawl right in. He'd never done anything like that, or led me to expect that he might.*

I suppose I was feeling rather jaunty about the way *You Bet Your Life* was accepted. It became the favorite show of the intellectuals, which was heartwarming, but it was also selling a lot of Elgin-American compacts. And since a substantial part of our audience was composed of children, which was terrific, I don't know who was buying them. The ratings, however, were still not much to write home about.

Nevertheless, when you're hot, you're hot. It became obvious to the broadcasting industry that this little quiz show might serve as a model for others. There was already talk that other comics were peddling their adaptations of our show to the networks.

Life magazine, in 1948, just as our first season at ABC was ending, went to a costume party. The picture that *Life* ran was taken on a staircase, and several Grouchos in mustache and cigar were pictured with the genuine, shaven article, who looked less like Groucho Marx than anyone else. That's because I was made up to look like Harpo.

During the party, I noticed a group of guests sitting in a corner. It wasn't until later that I discovered they were complaining about the upcoming Red purge of Hollywood. Of liberal bent and missionary zeal, some feared they'd unwisely lent their names to what were rapidly becoming unpopular causes. I confess I didn't worry too much about the situation at the time. I was happy at ending the first season of the show and looking forward to continuing it in the fall.

BERNIE SMITH: In those days radio shows had summer replacements. The big shows went on for thirty-nine weeks and then they would have a cheaper show in the summer. We had one the first year that was terrible, with a bunch of old vaudeville comedians. John Guedel and I had breakfast one morning. We were quite concerned. Something had to be done or our time slot was going to be shot, and we'd have to start building it all over again in the fall. "Why don't we use the shows again?" John asked. "Most people only hear the show once every three weeks. They go to a movie or something. All that wonderful stuff goes down the drain for two thirds of the audience." So we got to thinking. We thought it might work if we took the thirteen best shows from the previous season and ran them instead of a summer replacement. Actually, it was Guedel's idea.

John called ABC. A network vice-president came to his office. Of course the network was very negative. John said, "Do you fellows know that the average listener hears a show only once out of every 3.4 times that it's on?" The eyebrows of the vice-president shot up. "I never heard of such a thing," he said, "but it's logical and it makes sense." John says, "Well, that's the figure. So I think it would be wise and it would be safe to run our show again." So the vice-president went back to the network and got the okay, and that's how reruns started. After he left, I said to John, "Where did you get that figure? I never heard of this survey." With this real sheepish grin, John said, "I made it up."

In the eyes of some, to invent the singing commercial was bad enough. But to also invent the rerun—well, all I can say is that I'm glad Guedel was on my side. He was looking out for my best interests, which also happened to coincide with his.

It wasn't long before he started making other noises.

"Groucho," he told me one day, "the show is a success on ABC, but it's never going to be a smash unless we move it to one of the major networks. We're going to want to sell the show to television, but it's not going to go unless the ratings are higher."

Of course, I agreed. I never doubted that we had something extraordinary here, and this feeling was confirmed when I won the Peabody Award for 1948, given to me the following year by the University of Georgia School of Journalism.

"What's so funny about me winning an award?" I was quoted as saying, "And by the way, who's this fellow Peabody?"

But I was enormously pleased, as I was when in January of 1949 I was named the best quizmaster on the air. On the heels of Dewey's defeat by Truman, I quipped, "It just goes to show that a man with a mustache can get elected."

Eddie Cantor, when hearing of these honors, observed, "No wonder he's so good. He practices twenty-four hours a day."

> MORRIE RYSKIND: Groucho would be more pleased about receiving such awards than the rest of the boys. Groucho has an inferiority complex that is shared by an awful lot of people for no bloody reason: the idea he wasn't a college man. But I know an awful lot of guys that went to college who haven't read as much as Groucho.

Before I knew it, the move over was an accomplished fact. We began show number sixty-two on CBS, on October 5, 1949.

Elgin-American remained as our sponsor, as *You Bet Your Life* started its third year. "After a few helpings of Groucho," one of the trade papers reported, "it should be easy to understand why Elgin-American refused to give him his release so he could make another deal for twice his current stipend."

Music was an integral part of our show from the start, and

we would soon be hiring our third bandleader in as many years. I knew I'd have to promise that, from now on, I would sing on key. The first bandleader we'd hired had what it takes to become one of the greatest. Unfortunately, he took it with him after the first season to go out on his own. His name was Billy May.

Stanley Meyers succeeded him, and he was now opting for greener pastures.

JERRY FIELDING: I'd been in radio for quite a while with Kay Kyser as an arranger. In fact I was with him for almost six years. My first job as a leader was on the Jack Paar show, the summer replacement for Jack Benny in 1947. It was all the Lucky Strike family. I was twenty-three at the time.

A friend had recommended me for an album of children's records with Groucho Marx. We did them on seventy-eights at Radio Recorders. I'd never met him before. He liked them, though, and right after that he had me put on the show, which was at CBS then.

I remember the room we did it in, because it was the same room in which we did the Kyser and Paar shows.

When I took the show over, there was nothing to do. We played the questions, did the lead-ins and lead-outs, and that's all. It was a breeze. I was limited to ten men because that's all the budget we had, so we had no piano.

During the first month we were on CBS, the show shot to sixth in the ratings, and stayed at that level for some time. With the fantastic increase in ratings, Elgin-American found its sales multiplied so quickly that its manufacturing capacity couldn't keep up with demand. Al Gellman relinquished sponsorship of the show after the Christmas selling season. Another sponsor was gunning its motors in the wings.

With our seventy-fifth show ushering in the new year on January 4, 1950, DeSoto-Plymouth dealers became our sponsors. By every standard *You Bet Your Life* was now in the big time.

The major networks could see that its potential on television was great, and they began eagerly bidding to acquire the property from Guedel and me.

48

Newsweek, on May 15, unconsciously marked the start of the negotiations when it put me on the cover. In the accompanying story, "A Sharp Knife in Stale Cake," I was described as having reached the Withering Heights. Though I was grateful for the publicity, I don't think their routine was nearly as funny as mine.

BERNIE SMITH: At that time, NBC had all the top radio shows: Jack Benny, Burns and Allen, everybody. When television came along, William Paley, the chairman of the board of CBS, and his boys went in and raided NBC. They got all the guys away from NBC and put them on CBS, all in one year. NBC was really up against it. Our agency—Batten Barton Durstine and Osborn—had an office in Detroit. We were now being sponsored by DeSoto. They told me that one of the top people at CBS went up to Detroit. They went to the president of the DeSoto division of Chrysler and put a check for a million dollars on his desk. They said, "If you use your weight to have Groucho and Guedel put their show on CBS, that million dollars is yours." They swore this really happened. DeSoto knew they couldn't keep it anyway, and he couldn't operate that way or he'd get fired. So he just told the guy, "I want to keep Groucho and Guedel happy. Whatever they say, I'll do."

Incidentally, the DeSoto dealers were paying twenty-seven dollars out of each car sale to support the show.

Anyway, it was decided to put up the show for bids.

JOHN GUEDEL: We were all to meet at Gummo's house at Carmelita and Beverly Drive. Gummo and the William Morris agency were Groucho's agents. They were half and half, but Gummo handled the arrangements. We were supposed to meet both networks or have the bids from both networks. Mr. Paley came over. We said, "You're not supposed to be here. These are to be just bids. Then we're supposed to think about it and make a decision later today." The NBC people were supposed to be there to present their bid. I don't know why they weren't supposed to send it in advance too, but they said, "Please let us talk to you." There was a fellow named Joe McConnell who was president of NBC at the time. The airplane was late, and there was an electrical storm, so they didn't get to the Beverly Hills Hotel until midnight. Groucho says, "Come on, let's go. Let's settle with CBS. They're darn nice people." I said, "Groucho, we have to wait until the others get here. It's not their fault there's a storm and they're late." So he said all right.

We were sitting at Gummo's being sociable. I rose and excused myself. Paley rose and followed me, into the guest bath, and locked the door.

"Look," he said to me, "you're a Jew and I'm a Jew. We should stick together. You can't afford to sign with NBC."

But there were a couple of fellows at NBC named Sarnoff, who were also Jews, though they'd never tried to drill the fact into me.

I told Paley I wasn't pleased with his conversation.

BERNIE SMITH: Groucho told me later that he made up his mind right there. He wouldn't go with CBS if that was the way they did business. He's a very sensitive man in areas you don't expect.

I don't know who started circulating the stories that I'm all that wholesome and clean-cut. But if I ever track him down, you can bet somebody's going to be sued for slander.

Actually I'm a prude. When my brothers and I were kids starting out in vaudeville, the houses we played at had the same sign backstage: ANYONE SAYING HELL OR DAMN DURING A PERFORMANCE WILL BE IMMEDIATELY FIRED.

We didn't have sex and profanity to fall back on, so we had to fall back on our talents.

Today, we have a distinguished actor making a picture, showing him fornicating with his overcoat on. I don't think he even tipped his hat to his partner, and that's no way to treat a lady.

What we also learned was taste. There are certain things that are private and inviolate. And that's why I got mad at Paley.

JOHN GUEDEL: Paley said, "I'll wait outside." He sat on the steps in his tuxedo, because he was supposed to go to dinner at Andy's house. Charles Correll, you know, played Andy on Amos 'n' Andy. Finally I persuaded him to go on to dinner. We said we wouldn't make a deal with NBC that night, and only on the promise that we would meet them again the following morning would he leave. That's the tenacity of the chairman of the board of CBS. It shows you the inside of a guy when he wants something. He sent for Frank Stanton, the president of CBS, to come out on the airplane that night, and he was there the next morning.

The NBC fellows arrived at midnight . . . McConnell and two or three NBC executives and a lawyer. Joe McConnell sat down in a wicker chair on the lanai, where we were having the meeting. The floor was slippery. He leaned back and the chair went right over on its back too. He slid twenty feet right across the room. That was his opening, his so-called entrance into the meeting. We talked it over and told them we would let them know the next day.

We met at the office of Larry Beilenson the next morning and talked to CBS. Then we decided on NBC, because they had more to gain, and the money was very high. They didn't have any big shows. CBS was getting them all.

We were in Beilenson's office, talking pretty good-sized money. The office was on Wilshire. Everybody was in kind of a hurry to get it done. They'd ask, "Well, what about Paragraph Four?" We'd say, "That's okay." It involved twenty-thousand dollars or so. "And what about Paragraph Five?" We said that's okay too.

Do you know what we were doing? We were so concerned, because we were all parked in meter zones downstairs, and we wanted to get down there before the meters ran out. Nobody thought to stop and go down to fix them or to send somebody from the office down with some dimes. No one would admit until later what the real reason was for our hurry. We each got two-dollar tickets anyway.

While *You Bet Your Life* was ending its run at CBS, I signed to make a film for United Artists, *Love Happy,* which was released later that year. It was a terrible picture, and I've tried to blot it out of my mind.

One memory, however, lingers. The producer called me one day. "We have three girls here," he said. "Why don't you come and pick one out?" No, this wasn't part of some new giveaway program. I would be picking the girl who would be doing a sexy vignette in the picture.

Three girls were lined up in the producer's office when I

arrived the following day. Each was required to walk up and down the room. Then the three girls left the room.

"Which one do you like?" the producer asked.

"You must be crazy," I replied. "There's only one, as far as I'm concerned. The blonde."

The girl was signed for the part. For her one scene she wore a dress cut so low that I couldn't remember the dialogue. Very soon other men throughout the world would be suffering similar fevers, for the girl was Marilyn Monroe.

It was anticlimax, of course, that our last show at CBS, and our one-hundredth, ended our third season on June 28, 1950.

We would have the summer to get the show ready for a new network and a new medium, television.

An article in *The Billboard* firmed up the deal in the industry's eyes. It also widened them:

HOLLYWOOD, July 8.—Details of the recently concluded NBC–Groucho Marx deal, obtained by The Billboard *this week, reveal that NBC is guaranteeing Marx $760,000 annually over a ten-year period, and in addition, is paying him, when the program is on the air, $4,800 weekly for 39 weeks a year. But that's not all. On top of this sizable slab of loot, the network is cutting the comic in for 38 per cent of its profit on the* You Bet Your Life *package.*

NBC has also given John Guedel, packager of the program, a similar 10-year "annuity." Guedel is listed, according to insiders, for $225,000 annually over 10 years, plus $1,800 weekly as producer of the show. He, too, is cut in for 13 per cent of the net profits. Thus, between the 38 per cent given Groucho and Guedel's cut, NBC will retain 49 per cent of the net profits of the package sale, for AM or TV or both.

Not including annual pay hikes, said to call for $800 a week each year, NBC is guaranteeing Marx a reported minimum of $263,200 annually. Guedel, without including annual increases, is slated for $98,700 annual. The combined total to both is $361,900 annual—which means that over 10 years and allowing for pay hikes for both, NBC is on the books for around $4,000,000 in guarantees.

And that ain't all. NBC is paying Marx's legal fees. He buys his own food, tho.

That last sentence is what passes for scintillating wit in some quarters. But I could afford to be magnanimous, for I had quite a few quarters to work with.

As the program staff started thinking of television, they began to suggest all sorts of changes in my appearance. A brilliant young writer named Groucho Marx wrote about it in his 1959 best seller, *Groucho and Me*.

"The first thing they asked me was how I would dress. I told them I would wear a regular suit of clothes, sit on a high stool and question people about their lives just as I had been doing on radio.

"A blood brother of all the other obstructionists bobbed up and said, 'Mr. Marx, you realize this isn't radio. This is television, and television is just movies on a smaller screen. You've got to give them action. You can't just sit there like a bump on a log.' (This chap was a real wit.) 'You've got to give them that funny walk and leap around the stage,' he insisted.

" 'Rubbish,' I said.

" 'Rubbish! Rubbish!' he exclaimed, as he jumped up and down. 'What kind of an answer is that?' "

" 'Not a very good one,' I conceded, 'but then you're no Ring Lardner yourself.'

" 'You mean you're just going to sit on a stool and not move at all?' he demanded.

" 'Not a muscle,' I replied.

" 'But you can't do that,' he insisted.

" 'Now listen, you Brooks Brothers radical,' I said. 'I saw Sam Levenson the other night on TV. He wore a regular suit of clothes, stood in one spot and delivered a monologue. And when he finished, the audience yelled for more.'

"He had no answer to that. He just reached into his charcoal-gray coat pocket, pulled out two dry martinis, drained them and silently walked away, a beaten man."

I've never revealed this until now, but I added that if the sponsor and the network wanted to see me with a full head of hair there'd be the devil toupée.

NBC pulled out all the publicity stops. As part of the preparation, I was asked to write an article incorporating my views on television.

"I must say I find television very educational," I wrote. "The minute somebody turns it on, I go into the library and read a good book."

> EDWIN I. MILLS: When it appeared we were going to go on television, we began talking about how we were going to do a radio show on television.
>
> Actually, we never really went for the visual. Not unless it was a boy meets girl situation.

Show number 101, aired on NBC radio on October 4, 1950, and telecast on NBC the following night, marked the beginning of one of the happiest associations of my life. I had no regrets that we'd chosen to go with NBC.

> ROBERT DWAN: On the first television show, there was no appropriation for sets. There were drapes in the studio that we used to do the radio show in front of. It took us a couple of years to get an appropriation for sets. Toward the end of the run we got sliding panels that would move back if the contestant wanted to dance or whatever.
>
> This was the most static television show ever produced, but it didn't bother anyone.

> HY FREEDMAN: The only time we had any problem was the first few weeks after we went into television. The logistics were different. What should we do because it's a television show? One of the great touches was that Groucho was able to inject his little shtick. Even if he never contributed one thing to the format that we had, we would have a show.

> ROBERT DWAN: We had a lot of physical restrictions. Groucho always wore the same necktie and the same jacket. Incidentally, he's the only guy we ever designed a jacket for that looked good sitting down.

We had his tailored so that it didn't have that wrinkle at the back of the collar like you normally get. George always wore the same suit. The rules of the show for any one season always stayed the same.

There was a reason for all that. I could have the flexibility of taking any interview and making it any length, and then combining it with another interview, if necessary, that may have been filmed on a different evening. In this way I could put together good combinations of people. Groucho and John left me entirely alone on this, with no interference in the editing. I would really stockpile spots of contestants.

It was very easy to leave Bob Dwan alone, as well as Bernie Smith. They knew what they were doing, and Guedel and I didn't need to intrude. In fact, as soon as all the snags were ironed out, John made himself rather scarce around the studio. The team was operating at full efficiency, and was apparently content, for in the fifteen years we were on the air, there were only three major personnel changes.

ROBERT DWAN: We've never taken any particular credit for this, but we really invented the multicamera system. We wanted to be able to edit and to have Groucho talk to people and not have to stop. Videotape wasn't invented at this point. The quality of sixteen-millimeter film wasn't good then and there was no color television. The obvious thing was to shoot in thirty-five millimeter black and white film.

The cameras only carried a ten-minute load of film. I decided to use two cameras alongside each other at every position. There were two pointing at Groucho, two for close-ups of contestants, two for a two-shot that could pan from Groucho and the middle contestant to the two contestants, and two cameras that shot all three. I used a cameraman and an assistant at each position. Another man was used to load film on all the cameras. One of each pair of cameras would run simultaneously from the four positions. At the end of nine and a half minutes the second set would start going, and this set would be succeeded by the original cameras at the end of another nine and a half minutes. Each pair of cameras would shoot one and a half hours in all, and I could edit with absolute freedom.

I always had a close-up picture of Groucho, no matter what he did. I could edit to get at the exact moment when he started his reaction.

We started with an elaborate system of lights to establish synchronization. We finally evolved to a simple system where the editor overlapped the film of each pair of cameras.

HY FREEDMAN: Our preparation has become the standard for all the talk shows. It was not only that, but also the taping. I must say that's a great technique. It's a combination of everything: Groucho, the selection of contestants, the preparation, and editing and keeping the best.

ROBERT DWAN: We had a device directly behind the contestants which worked like an overhead projection at a bowling alley. Only Groucho saw it. Written on it were the opening and closing jokes. Because nobody on God's green earth is going to be able on immediately meeting you to pull out a precise interview question that is going to work. So when we got the people we spent a lot of time talking to them.

Sometimes the time spent with them was not long enough. We weren't too far along in our first season on NBC when a male contestant appeared. He was talking about his most embarrassing experience. "I was rooming with a three-hundred-pound fellow," he told me. "And the bedroom caught fire. In my panic I put on the big fellow's trousers and shoes. I was coming down the ladder when a shoe came loose. I tried to retrieve it, and I dropped the trousers. There was a crowd of five hundred people below, and they could all see my predicament."

The resulting uproar was immense, and though the anecdote was clipped by Bob Dwan, our resident blue nose, the laugh was nevertheless aired. Hundreds of times. For it was that bring-the-house-down response which was used for years by NBC on laugh tracks for other shows.

But little matter. We had plenty laughs to spread around.

BERNIE SMITH: There's a show business axiom I always adhered to with Groucho's encouragement. George M. Cohan said, "Nobody will ever leave the room when there's a pretty girl there." So, nobody was going to leave the television set either. Women like to see pretty girls too, because they like to see how they dress.

I never knew before now that policies such as that had to be formulated, that one week we would have dogs and the next we'd blossom out with the first in a long series of Miss Americas. There was never a time that we didn't have pretty girls on the show. It was one of the stipulations of my contract.

MARION POLLOCK: I started on the show just after it went on TV. I was assigned to dig up people who would be interesting. Later I got promoted to write all the questions. They said, "You've been promoted to vice-president in charge of the quiz." At no raise in pay.

I wrote the questions until the bitter end. I read extensively in every single reference book: almanacs, histories, encyclopedias, any compendium of factual knowledge . . . particularly for the big question. This had to be timeless.

You couldn't have any questions that mentioned a competing product. In other words, I couldn't ask a question about the Chrysler Building, even though DeSoto was a Chrysler product.

We had about twenty-four categories to submit to contestants before the show, each with sample questions. People would get desperate if they couldn't find one, and at the last minute they'd pick General Information, which was the hardest. It was the downfall for many.

The contestants never met until right before the show. If one of them insisted on a category and blew it, you could see the dirty look from the other contestant.

There were some categories preferred by the contestants. One was naming the state from a list of cities. Another was popular music. The staff didn't like that much because it cost money, for we had to pay for music rights. If the category was sports, the man always picked it.

When you see a couple and one does all the work, it's only because he insisted on getting the opportunity.

ROBERT DWAN: There was a great advantage to having the contestants stand behind a microphone. It offered them a little security. They would just walk in and stand behind the mike. Instead of having them toe the mark, we had them stand on some floor mats, and as long as they stayed on them, we knew they were in the right place for the cameras to pick them up.

It wasn't a pilgrimage to Mecca, but it was just as religious

57

a trek I took every Wednesday night to the NBC studios at Sunset and Vine over the next eleven years. When we started on television, there were 3.1 million sets in homes in the United States. Within five years this amount would increase tenfold to 32 million, and during that period *You Bet Your Life* remained in the Top Ten.

The show had been on television only a couple of months when word came from England, and it was as great an honor as I'd ever received. Blanche Patchy, a private secretary, in a book about her famous employer, said George Bernard Shaw felt the greatest actor of his time was Groucho Marx!

If this was the case, then I'd better live up to that estimation. Reporting once a week at seven thirty, for a maximum of one and a half hours before the television cameras, seemed insufficient for a man of my newfound standing.

As one of television's newest stars, and despite the abysmally bad *Love Happy* and *Mr. Music*, which I'd made the previous year, I again found myself inundated by movie scripts.

Howard Hughes was then head of RKO, and I signed with him to costar with Jane Russell and Frank Sinatra in *Double Dynamite*. The title had nothing to do with the story.

The picture was dutifully made. I suspected during its making that it wouldn't reach the epic grandeur of *Gone with the Wind*. I was right.

A while later, Hughes called to ask if I would promote another RKO picture. "If you do some publicity for us, I'll fly you around the world in my airplane," he said.

I agreed. He flew the coop soon after. Nevertheless, I still plan to collect on this past due bill. I have asked Judge Crater to come along for the ride.

JERRY FIELDING: When we moved over to NBC I was very much involved in politics and all kinds of crusades. That's something I'm happy to say I never stopped doing. I was very young.

I was twenty-three, I'd been almost seven years in the business. I kind of knew what I was about by the time I got that far, so I felt justified in making certain demands.

One of the things that bugged me most was that we had two unions in this town, a black one and a white one. It wasn't true in New York. The white union had a higher scale than the black union and a higher death benefit, and a lot of other things. In other words, there were first- and second-class types of musicians.

There had never been a black musician on the West Coast playing network shows on the radio. When we moved over to NBC we made some changes. I had involved myself with people I knew, and since I was in a position to do something about it, I joined to form an amal- gamation committee to break this law down. We were going to put two black guys on the Groucho Marx show. Oddly enough, the leadership of the black union came down on us like a ton of bricks, because they didn't want an amalgamation. If we took the black guys in, they were out of a job. So we didn't get any help from the black union.

Buddy Collette, I guess, was our first token black. Groucho felt the idea was very good, and when I got noise from NBC, I went to him and he backed me up pretty strongly. But at the time I was told in no uncertain terms that if I kept this up, they were going to get me.

The amalgamation finally happened, and pretty soon the black one went out of business. It was on account of the Groucho Marx show that this happened. Otherwise, there'd still be two unions here.

We had been a smash during our first season, and six months after we started the television version of *You Bet Your Life,* the Academy of Television Arts and Sciences, in its third annual awards, named me Outstanding Television Per- sonality of 1950. I was asked by the press what I thought of winning an Emmy the first year I was eligible for the award. I responded, "I deserve it. I've been a good father to all my children and a good husband to all my wives."

BERNIE SMITH: We were NBC's top-rated show for three or four years, and we were in the Top Ten for the whole run. Underneath it all was a lot of thought. When it first started, I asked myself, "Whom are we trying to appeal to?" I did some pretty profound thinking about this. I realized the audience was made up of a whole lot of minority groups. We're all minority groups. So, very deliberately and very care- fully in making up the shows, I would always make sure I had one Irishman, one German, one Oriental, or some ethnic group. By the end of the first year, we covered everybody. And we tried to put them in a sympathetic situation, so that all the people of that minority would say, "That's my boy up there. That's a great show. He won some money. He's smart."

ROBERT DWAN: Did the contestants feel put upon? They did not. They came knowing what was going to happen to them, and it was such a popular show. It was a great coup to be on the thing. You were now instantly, nationally, famous, and besides, you could win a little money. The money was unimportant, but we would try to be pretty consistent. We once had a Congressional Medal of Honor winner go broke on the quiz, and Norman Krasna bawled Groucho out for not letting the guy win.

GEORGE FENNEMAN: Of course, from the show I got all the DeSoto commercials. I became their spokesman for eight or nine years. I also did Dragnet during the same time. Nobody knows that. I'm the voice that says, "The story you are about to see is true. The names have been changed to protect the innocent." Jack Webb and I met in San Francisco, and his loyalty has carried over. Almost everything he does he calls me in to do a good luck line, which is also a good luck check. I'm still getting paid for Dragnet. It's running two times a day syndicated.

ROBERT DWAN: After I got all finished editing the show we might need to shoot some pickup scenes. There were a lot of mysterious things in that editing. I saw one the other day. There was Prince Monolulu, the racetrack tout from Ethiopia, a crazy African guy. And we said, "We're running out of time. You gotta come back next week." And the next week he came back. Well, that was all done on one evening. It was one long interview, and I couldn't fit it all into one program. So we picked a point. I guess at the time I must have had him make another entrance.

We might do pickup shots six weeks later, so that the different segments I'd put together would come out right. George Fenneman was marvelous at this . . . his intonation, his decibel level, his whole approach. He was that kind of consistent performer.

Then there were also the problems with the secret word. Let's say the word for the night is "foot." I might want to put it together with a spot from another show, only they happen to say "foot" on this segment. I'd have to invent a whole different secret word, one that none of the cou-

60

ples had used, and stick that at the top of the show. I had a stockpile of ducks coming with different secret words.

And they say that television is just a big sausage factory! Where else but on our show could you find such spontaneity and spark? So don't tell me that the show was a breeze to perform, and don't say I'm not as good an actor as Shaw described. I have dozens of takes and retakes to prove otherwise.

Our second television season opened with an intramural flap. A young man, John Anson Ford, was a contestant. BBD&O, DeSoto's advertising agency, said we couldn't have a Ford on a DeSoto show, and they made him change his name. The young man was the son of a Los Angeles County supervisor, and it didn't sit well with many people, myself included. Television, if nothing else, has raised absurdity to a fine art.

I had already perfected it in my previous incarnations as star of stage and screen. What may be absurd to some will be hilarious to others. Don't ask me why.

If I may digress, now seems as good a time as any to offer some Marxist theory.

There is no formula for comedy. There's only practice, and more practice. My brothers and I worked in vaudeville for twenty-two years. We started in Small Time, which meant we performed four shows a day for five days, and five shows a day on Saturday and Sunday. We played split weeks in two cities, which means we moved from one city to another in the middle of the week.

For example, we played three days in Burlington, Iowa, caught the train overnight, and played the following four days in Waterloo. This was very hard work: four a day for five days equals twenty shows; five a day for two days equals ten more shows, for a total of thirty shows per week. In this case we played twelve shows in Burlington and eighteen shows in Waterloo.

Why, outside the necessity of sheer survival, did we do

this? We all wanted to be the best, the most perfect, the most flawless, the funniest that we could possibly be. Nobody else can be funny for you. You've got to be funny yourself.

There didn't seem to be the compulsion then for one comic to top the other. We did not want to take from some other person or be better than him. Who can possibly be the judge of that? The judgment is the laughter that comes from the audience. We wanted to know we were good, and funny, within ourselves.

We were all constantly striving to improve ourselves, to get more laughs from the audience; to understand and learn how to get more laughs from the audience. We (and by that I mean my brothers, as well as Jack Benny, George Burns, Phil Harris, Frank Fay, and many others who were cohorts in those days) tried to help one another. It was a very good way to live.

There was no television in those days, and only the big cities had silent movie houses. So entertainment was live on stage. This is the reason why there were so many shows a day, and why we of that era had a built-in advantage of perfecting our craft, which entertainers of today do not.

We learned the importance of delivery. One cannot pull phrases at random and sling them together in a sloppy manner with no consideration as to style. The suspenseful building of the structure toward the punch line will, hopefully, make the audience respond with laughter. These phrases must be carefully chosen and planned in order to gain the audience's response. It takes many years on the stage, in front of a live audience, to learn this art, to learn how to deliver those carefully chosen words in the most casual, artless way. Finally, if you are dedicated enough, you learn, subconsciously, HOW TO TELL A STORY.

If you're at it long enough, then maybe you too will have your humor analyzed by *Time* magazine, as mine was done in a cover story on December 31, 1951.

"His quiz program (NBC, Wed., 9 p.m. E.S.T.; TV,

Thurs., 8 p.m.), *You Bet Your Life,* is now well into its fifth season. When one of the contestants, a pretty and shapely high school math teacher, explained that geometry is the study of lines, curves and surfaces, Groucho gave his celebrated leer and panted, 'Kiss me, fool!' The audience reaction threatened to blow the back out of the broadcasting theater. Groucho's jokes sound far funnier than they read afterwards. But there are exceptions, such as the one when he asked a tree surgeon on his program, 'Tell me, Doctor, did you ever fall out of a patient?'

"With Groucho, delivery is almost everything. An old line of his, 'The air is like wine tonight,' used to make audiences choke with laughter a couple of decades ago. When he would simply say, 'I think I'll go out and get a cold towel,' then start for the wings with the queer, buzzardy shuffle he used for a walk, it would leave the audiences strangling. Because nowadays he seldom moves from the high stool he sits on during broadcasts, the buzzardy shuffle is gone. But the rest of the delivery is still there, as good or better than ever: the perfectly timed twitch of the brows; the play of the luminous brown eyes—now rolling with naughty thoughts, now staring through the spectacles with only half-amused contempt; the acidulous, faint smile; the touch of fuming disgust in the voice ('That's as shifty an answer as I've ever heard'); above all, the effrontery.

"Groucho's other superb professional asset is his lightning ability to ad-lib jokes. His mind is like a panful of popcorn kernels with heat underneath: one ad lib bursts, and the air is filled with popcorn. *You Bet Your Life,* his current show, simultaneously tape-recorded for radio and filmed for television, is not exactly a simon-pure ad-lib performance. Contestants are chosen in advance, made to fill out questionnaires about themselves, and coached for an hour and a half before facing Groucho. But Groucho is still a better field shot than any other ad-libber, and shows it by shooting from the hip at these clay pigeons."

63

I like publicity as much as the next entertainer, and I was happy to be on *Time*'s cover, but I thought the analysis was excessive, for you simply can't intellectualize about comedy. The only thing I liked was their mention of my luminous brown eyes. I just couldn't see how anyone can suitably describe anything so fragile as humor. I've had a lifetime as a comedian, and I would never have tried.

Let me tell you a favorite anecdote of mine.

A man goes up to a box office in a small town.

"What's playing tonight?" he asks.

"Tickets are one dollar," the man at the box office replies.

"I'll take one," the fellow says. "But tell me. What is it—sad or high-kicking?"

That's all of show business: sad or high-kicking.

The same month as the *Time* cover story also saw the birth of our first "civilian star" on the show. She was a very unlikely prospect. Her name was Anna Badovnic, a jolly Yugoslavian who appeared with a Hollywood furrier as her partner.

When you have a natural comic talent such as this, you feed the straight lines and stand back. Such was the case as I started my interview with Mrs. Badovnic:

GROUCHO
How do you spell your name, Anna?

ANNA
A—n—n—a . . .

GROUCHO
How do you spell Badovnic?

ANNA
B—a—d—o—v—n—i—c . . . Okay.

GROUCHO
You have a very interesting accent, Mrs. Badovnic. Where were you born?

ANNA
Uhh—Pennsylvania—near Uniontown. I was five years old and I went to Yugoslavia.

64

GROUCHO

There's something fishy going on here. . . . Let's talk about furs. Where's your shop?

MITCHELL

Mitchell Furs. It's on Hollywood Boulevard near Normandie.

GROUCHO

How is the fur business?

MITCHELL

It's holding up very well.

GROUCHO

Can you say as much for your fur coats?

MITCHELL

Yes, I believe so.

GROUCHO

I see. Your business is holding up and your coats are holding up. How about your customers—they're being held up too, aren't they? After all, he is in the skin game. That's only a joke. How did you like it, Bernard?

MITCHELL

Well, it's not a very good joke for the fur business.

GROUCHO

It's not a very good joke for show business. . . . Anna, will you tell us how you met your husband.

ANNA

Yeah. When I was five years old, I go to Yugoslavia. Then when I was fifteen, my mother was looking for my husband.

GROUCHO

Your mother was looking for your husband? How long were you married by that time?

ANNA

My mother was born in a village—Badovnic. Badovnic village, and Badovnic was husband. She was born there and she find a husband named Badovnic.

GROUCHO

Your husband was named Badovnic and your mother was looking for him?

ANNA

Yeah. Hungarian village was named Badovnic too.

GROUCHO

Why didn't you marry the village? . . . You had two husbands named Badovnic?

ANNA

Yes. I was twelve years with the first one. And when I come
to this country he run away. I never see him. My mother
found him. I was just fifteen years old and—

GROUCHO

What did she do? Did she pluck just any boy out of the
crowd?

ANNA

I was fifteen years old. I don't know. I have nothing to say. I
was too young. Now I know how to pick them.

GROUCHO

It's never too late. Somewhere in Michigan there must be a
village named Badovnic. What about this village named Badovnic?

ANNA

In Yugoslavia.

GROUCHO

There's a village named Badovnic?

ANNA

Two! The whole village. Badovnic and people named too.
(At this point the duck came down, for the secret word was
"people.")

GROUCHO

Well, you said Badovnic, so you win fifty dollars. Anyone
who says Badovnic on this show wins. Well, I don't understand. You say there was a whole village named Badovnic.

ANNA

Yeah. Whole village. Everybody last name Badovnic.

GROUCHO

That's pretty confusing, isn't it? Where does the mailman
know where to bring the mail?

66

ANNA

Everyone has a first name, like John or Pete or Mike. Like that.

GROUCHO

I see. All the last names are the same . . . and the town is the same thing. And they have two Badnovic villages?

ANNA

Yes. And the other one not far, but not together.

GROUCHO

I see. How did you come to America?

ANNA

I come with my husband. Badovnic.

GROUCHO

I thought your mother was chasing your husband.

ANNA

No. I was married when my mother pick him.

GROUCHO

Oh. And then you came to America, and brought the village with him?

ANNA

And then my first husband when I come here he run away.

GROUCHO

Your first husband ran away? And went back to Badovnic?

ANNA

Then I found another Badovnic.

GROUCHO

Where was your mother while this was going on?

ANNA

My mother was in Yugoslavia.

GROUCHO

So the second time you picked out your own Badovnic. Did you find your second Badovnic an improvement over your first Badovnic?

ANNA

It was better. Yeah.

67

Well, ladies, be sure to tune in tomorrow for another exciting chapter of *Anna's Other Badovnic.*

ANNA

Yes, but my second husband I call Pete. And eight kids . . . three family kids I raise . . . mine, my husband and me, and my man both together.

GROUCHO

Well, you certainly make an unusual couple . . . and anything else I might add would be gilding the Badovnic. I want you to take my advice and visit your DeSoto-Plymouth dealer—Joe Badovnic. Now we're going to play *You Bet Your Life* and—

ANNA

I don't know how to play *You Bet Your Life.*

GROUCHO

Then we're going to play *You Bet Your Badovnic* instead.

When I finished my encounter with Anna I felt like I'd been part of an Abbott and Costello routine. But at last I knew who's on first. Badovnic.

That is, until the question "Who's on first?" was asked again and the answer was Groucho Marx—in the witness box.

> *JOHN GUEDEL: NBC bought the show from Groucho and me lock, stock, and barrel. It was a capital gains deal. The government, however, felt it wasn't. They claimed a partnership cannot sell an asset. So we went to court, and it took us three or four years. It became a test case, and we won. And now there's Marx-Guedel versus the government, which states that a partnership can sell a capital asset.*

I took my attorney, Larry Beilenson, to New York. He'd written fifty questions they would probably ask me, and I had prepared my replies.

As I got up on the witness stand, I noticed that the judge had a radio under his desk and he was listening to the ball game. He was more interested in the ball game.

The government lawyer asked some questions. None of them were on Beilenson's list. This was one other quiz that wasn't fixed.

"I don't understand," I replied to him. I turned to the judge with an aside. "When he was studying law I was studying show business. I don't understand his questions."

The judge said, "Mr. Marx, just answer yes or no."

"How can I," I replied, "if I don't understand the questions? That's why I have my lawyer. He's reputed to be a great lawyer . . . unless he loses this case." Spectators laughed, and Beilenson took his hat and attaché case and walked out of the courtroom.

He did come back later, though, and he won the case that set the precedent.

And speaking of precedents, it wasn't long after that that I caused an international incident by unintentionally insulting the Precedent of Mexico.

Several MGM stars, Harpo and myself included, though we were stars emeritus, were invited to go to Mexico City for a movie festival. It was the summer of 1952.

We were having a great time, being tequilaed and tortillaed (that's how they wine and dine in Mexico).

Our translator, one evening, informed us that we were invited to meet the President the following day.

Knowing a thing or two about Latin-American politics, I asked, "How will we know if he'll still be President tomorrow?"

It was bad enough that the Mexicans didn't see the humor of the question, but neither did the other MGM stars. The rest of the company after that didn't want anything to do with us.

Harpo, his wife, Susan, and I were forced to fend for ourselves from that point on.

BERNIE SMITH: As I said, Groucho coined the Grant's Tomb idea. And he was at the bullfights in Mexico City one year. There were one hundred thousand people there, and the guy is goring the bull or the bull is goring the guy, and everybody's excited. Groucho couldn't

69

stand it. He got up to leave, and from way on the other side of the stadi-um somebody yells, "Hey, Groucho! Who's buried in Grant's Tomb?"

This reminded me that I had a new season of *You Bet Your Life* to prepare for and we returned to the United States.

We started our third season on television with a controversy that raged for days. It would ultimately involve some of the greatest minds of the civilized world.

It all aired on September 3, 1952.

> *ROBERT DWAN: A fellow was in my office the other day. A man named Art Lavove. He was on with a tall girl—a six-foot tip-topper or something. The big question was: "What Shakespearean character was in these plays:* Henry IV, Henry V, *and* The Merry Wives of Windsor?" *And he answered "Pistol." Groucho said, "No, it's Falstaff." Now it turns out this guy was right. Falstaff was not in* Henry V. *We got Laurence Olivier and Ralph Richardson and seven or eight different authorities and had him come back and clear the whole thing up.*

> *MARION POLLOCK: That was the one question that got us the most press. Lavove insisted Falstaff was not in* Henry V. *We insisted he was, for he was mentioned as dying offstage. We went to Shakespearean experts. They were divided. Some insisted Falstaff was in all three plays; others disagreed. But "Pistol" was also a correct answer, and we paid the contestants off. I thought all the publicity was delightful.*

A few weeks later we had a guest performer on the show who was so talented and so winsome that we just had to keep bringing her back. She would ultimately be on the show a dozen times or more.

It was on October 18 when my daughter Melinda finally got her act together. She was all of five.

> *MELINDA MARX BERTI: I remember very well being put out in front of the entire television world and being expected to come up with a marvelous performance. I remember on this first performance that I sang a song and did a little dance with my feet.*

70

When I was very little I had fun singing and dancing, and I would have done it in an alley. But I quickly became aware of tremendous pressure. During later times it became very intense and uncomfortable and something I didn't want to do at all.

Groucho has his own fantasy about it, which is fine, but he never asked me if I enjoyed it or wanted it. He'll deny that he was a stage mother, but I'm afraid it's true. It was something that was expected of me: clean your room, do well in school, and give a good performance on the television show.

I might add that Melinda was a much better entertainer than she was as a room cleaner. She appeared to be having a whale of a time on the show, and I encouraged her to appear. Being your typical proud and doting father, I wanted to show off her gifts to the world. I might have been a bit smug about her talent, which was obviously inherited. I was tickled with the idea that a third generation of performing Marxes was being introduced to the public.

I didn't sense until later that Melinda was unhappy being on the show. On the other hand I was quite aware that the sponsor was quite happy to have her. Our ratings were still in the Top Ten, and "the secret word" had already passed into the American idiom. DeSoto was doing very well by me, and vice versa.

JOHN GUEDEL: Very few people have problems with sponsors when you have good ratings. The problems you have with them are when you're marginal, and they say let's get this thing going. We were more or less in the driver's seat, because it didn't cost them a hell of a lot of money and it was delivering very well. Groucho was very cooperative. He'd film things like "Tell them Groucho sent you." It was in vogue right from the start.

GEORGE FENNEMAN: We'd been making some commercials for DeSoto at Universal Studios, and we broke for lunch. Groucho and I and three or four agency guys were sitting down having lunch. A woman came over to the table—they allowed civilians in the Commissary—and said, "Groucho Marx! Let me have your autograph." She leaned over the table and he said, "I'll do it only if you show us your tits again." To a perfect stranger, right? We were all sitting there . . . Oh, God, no! Well of course she blanched and he gave her his autograph. After she left, I said, "Groucho, why did you do that?" Because, you know, you're dying. She wasn't especially beautiful, nor especially young. And he said, "That woman undoubtedly came from Iowa. She has to go back to Iowa and all her life she'll remember what I said to her."

(I'm not one to dispute the words of other people, but I don't remember this episode at all. It is, without doubt, the product of George's overactive imagination.)

Another time we were waiting for a table at the Brown Derby and a very attractive woman came up behind us. Groucho turned to her. "Are you alone?" She said, "Yes." And Groucho said, "Then there must be something terribly wrong with you."

You know, I'm basically shy. I had to turn away. I've been in the wrong business all these years, I guess. Some people say I have good manners and that I have regard for others and don't want to hurt anybody. What I guess I'm saying is that I like to be liked. It's a curse. Like when I'm out to dinner. I never tip. I always overtip. Maybe I overtipped on the show too. But it seemed to work. Whatever my personality is, people out there thought of me as a nice guy and this man as slightly evil.

Sometimes Groucho's baiting technique used to make me cringe a little, but the contestants never seemed to care. They just barreled right on, and were oblivious, it seemed, to what he was saying.

Yet I can't impress on you too much what it means to be working with a legend. I was thirty years old and working with this man who was sixty at the time, who'd been the biggest star of all the media.

I never intended to be cruel to contestants. What evolved was a characterization with which we could both be comfortable. I learned early never to play to the audience. I played directly to the contestants.

BERNIE SMITH: Why is Groucho sharp and caustic and not insulting? Because I never thought he was insulting. He always had a twinkle in his eye. He was never a big strong boy. He was always kind of frail. And he grew up in a very tough neighborhood in New York, where the kids were pretty physical. In a fight he didn't have a prayer.

72

The only protection he had was his wit. He would get a friend or foe off balance by saying something. They'd do a double-take. Before they could start to work on him he'd get to work on them. That was his defense mechanism. It kept developing. He's exploited it and he's made a lot of money out of it.

The beauty of Jack Benny's humor is that he never pushes. I use the present tense, even though Jack has passed on, because his comedy influence is still much with us.

I'm the antithesis of that, the wise guy, and it's the contestants who are in trouble. We're both equally sympathetic. The audience likes Jack and the audience likes me.

I would be appalled if anyone took me seriously and thought I actually am the unlovable curmudgeon they've seen on the television screen.

A comedian will never be a star unless he *is* loved. That is why Don Rickles will never be a star, even though he is a star. It may be therapeutic to let out venom and hostility. It may even be funny. But it's not the type of material that will make his name live through the ages.

There were times when I worried about the image I presented to the public. Certainly the name of Groucho didn't help.

George Fenneman probably took more nonsense from me than anybody, yet he survived. I don't see that he's turned to a whimpering mass of jelly. I hope I look that good when I'm his age.

GEORGE FENNEMAN: In the early days Groucho got me confused, or at least the schools Bob Dwan and I went to confused, so that he had me going to Stanford and Bob going to State. Then when I started doing the quiz, and having to compile answers from the numbers, I made a lot of mistakes. People had a hundred dollars and they were allowed to bet any part of it. They'd bet thirty-seven twenty-seven. Well, by the time I'd written down thirty-seven twenty-seven they'd given the answer and Groucho asks, "How much do they have?" I'd have no idea. And then it became that, to be that stupid, you have to go to Stanford. Well, that went on and every time I'd make a mistake of any

*kind, Groucho would say, "You know, that boy's a Stanford graduate."
And it built and built. Well, first I started getting letters from San
Francisco State people, saying they thought it was lousy that I lied
about the school I went to, and that I'd picked Stanford because it has
more class than San Francisco State. So I got in trouble with the alum-
ni. Then I'd go to a party and I'd run into people who went to Stanford. They'd say, "I think my brother was in your biology class at Stanford." So I'm now a man without a school. I told all this to Groucho
and he said, "I'll fix it tonight on the show." So naturally when we got
on the show, he says, "George, I understand you've been lying about the
school you went to." I tried to explain that I went to San Francisco
State and not Stanford. He said, "What was that school again?" I
said, "San Francisco State College in San Francisco." He said,
"There's no such school. You just made that up. You know you'd have
to go to Stanford to be that stupid."*

All through our third season on television, our show
stayed at about eighth on the Nielsen ratings. The show was
hot, but it wasn't red-hot, until a hot tamale was recruited as
a contestant.

*EDWIN I. MILLS: We were going our greatest. The show caught
fire. I was out searching for personalities. I traveled all over the United States. I found some beauties in the Ozarks. We'd fly these contestants to Hollywood and put them up in a hotel. But that's all we'd pay.
They'd have to honestly win more. Everything was close to the vest. We
had no budget to do otherwise. And yet the people died to get on. I don't
know what it was. They certainly received no guarantees.*

*Dixie Thompson, a girl on the Walter O'Keefe show, told me about
one fellow, a clever Mexican who had knocked about the fringes of
show business. I tried to contact him. His name was Gonzalez.*

*RAMIRO G. GONZALEZ: Well, I'm from San Antonio, Tex-
as . . . little town . . . and Walter O'Keefe came to do a telethon
for palsy—United Cerebral Palsy. I was working at WOAI, not as a
disc jockey. I was picking up the cables for the cameras. I was labor,
you know.*

*Walter O'Keefe put on a beautiful show, and Dagmar, you know,
big Dagmar, was on the show too. They started doing the show. And I*

74

was looking at the show. I wanted to be in the show, but I couldn't. I was making nine ninety-five a week at WOAI, and I have three kids and a wife. I also worked in bars. I did my own act. I play skillets, frying pans. But I didn't have no money. I never went to school. I didn't know how to read or write.

I was picking up the cables for the cameras. So then Walter O'Keefe told me, "Do you work?" I say, "Yeah, I can work if you let me work." He said, "I don't know, I'm not the boss." Around three or four o'clock in the morning they ran out of acts. So Walter O'Keefe told me, "Go ahead, kid, and work." So I worked. I played my act. I danced with Dagmar. The telethon made one hundred and twenty-five thousand dollars.

Walter O'Keefe said, "Hey, kid, you're all right. Why don't you go to California?" I said, "No, I don't want to go. That's too far." He said, "You interested?" I said, "Sure, I'm interested in working, but I don't make no money." Walter O'Keefe told me, "Listen, kid. You did a good job. I'm going to see what I can do for you."

Walter O'Keefe told Groucho, "Listen, there's a boy but you gotta send him the money because he don't make no money." Groucho sent me three hundred dollars to catch a plane.

And I'm going to tell you something. You'll never believe this. I never saw Groucho on television. I didn't have no television. Never in my life did I see the show. I used to call him Groocho . . . Groocho. And when they sent me the money to come over there, I went to tell my boss. "I'm going to work with Groocho . . . Groocho . . . I don't know his name." He said, "Godalmighty! Can't you say Groucho?" I say, "Yeah, that's the man I'm going to work with. Groucho!"

I never seen three hundred dollars in my life. That's what they gave me to catch a plane. I put two hundred dollars in the bank and I catch a bus. I came with a T-shirt, a pair of Levi's, and tennies. And I went there to NBC, at Sunset and Vine. So when I went there, I went to the guard. He looked at me and say, "Just a minute." So he called. They said, "Yeah, send him over." I don't know who was looking at me. "You got a suit?" I say, "No, that's all I got." So he say, "Well, see what you can do." I had a sister here and she get me a suit, and I put that suit on and came back. Man say, "Don't be afraid. Just go in there and do the show. If Groucho say anything, don't get mad. It's all in fun."

So I went in. I just played it straight. I never did in my life a show in English. First time. I always work in Spanish.

The show was recorded on January 7, 1953. Gonzalez came on with Sally Neidlinger, an attractive young girl who worked in a ski shop. I asked her a few perfunctory questions and then turned to the young Mexican.

GROUCHO

Mr. Ramiro G. Gonzalez. Is that you?

GONZALEZ

Sí, señor.

GROUCHO

Sí, sí! Señor! . . . Ramiro G. Gonzalez. What does the G stand for, Ramiro?

GONZALEZ

Gonzalez.

GROUCHO

I know. Ramiro G. Gonzalez. What does the G stand for?

GONZALEZ

Ramiro Gonzalez Gonzalez.

GROUCHO

What are you—twins?

GONZALEZ

No.

GROUCHO

Are you pinch-hitting for your father?

GONZALEZ

No. I'm Ramiro Gonzalez Gonzalez because my father before she married my mother he was Gonzalez.

GROUCHO

Would you give me that once more?

GONZALEZ

My father was Gonzalez before he married my mother. My mother was Gonzalez before she married my father.

GROUCHO

Then they were crazy to get married? . . . What does your wife call you—Ramiro or Gonzalez?

GONZALEZ

She call me Pedro.

76

GROUCHO

That's the easy way, huh? I'll just call you Gonzalez Gonzalez
Pedro Gonzalez Sam Gonzalez.

GONZALEZ

Everybody call me Pedro.

GROUCHO

Where are you from, Mr. Gonzalez Gonzalez—Walla Walla?

GONZALEZ

San Antonio, Te-has.

GROUCHO

What's that?

GONZALEZ

San Antonio, Te-has.

GROUCHO

What do you do for a living?

GONZALEZ

I work at the WOAI radio station. I just drive a station wag-
on, pick up some copies, and sometime I take money and
take it to the station . . . that's all I do.

GROUCHO

You're married.

GONZALEZ

Oh, yes.

GROUCHO

How long have you been married?

GONZALEZ

Nine years. *(Makes a face)*

GROUCHO

Was your wife named Gonzalez before you married her?

GONZALEZ

No.

GROUCHO

How did you meet Mrs. Gonzalez Gonzalez?

GONZALEZ

She was working in San Antonio in an old theater. She was a
dancer. And I had a friend, and then, she took me to her

77

backstage, and then she gave me a good look, and I gave her another good look—

GROUCHO

What kind of a look did you give this girl when you met her backstage? Can you give us a sample?

GONZALEZ

Well, I just—can I look at her? *(Points to Sally)*

GROUCHO

Give her a look.

(Gonzalez does a Groucho-like leer, complete with eyebrows)

GROUCHO

Did that have any effect on you, Sally?

SALLY

Well . . . I looked back.

GROUCHO

Well, I'm curious about your courtship, Pedro. Didn't her mother object because her daughter was so young?

GONZALEZ

Well, she object sometimes, you know. I remember one time I went to see my girlfriend, to take her a serenade.

GROUCHO

You took her a serenade?

GONZALEZ

Yeah, like I saw in the movies. So I took a serenade to her. And then I got my guitar to sing her a song. When I was singing the song, I saw the window open, and I thought it was my girlfriend who was going to give me a nice good night kiss.

GROUCHO

And she was upstairs and you were downstairs?

GONZALEZ

Yes, sir.

GROUCHO

Well, how could she kiss you if she was upstairs and you were downstairs?

GONZALEZ

I climb up.

78

GROUCHO

She was younger than you. She could have climbed down.

GONZALEZ

And then the window open, and I thought it was my girl-friend, but, no, it was her mother. She throw me a pail of water.

GROUCHO

She threw a pail of water on you?

GONZALEZ

Yes.

GROUCHO

What were you singing—"Kiss of Fire"?

GONZALEZ

No.

GROUCHO

What were you singing? Do you remember?

GONZALEZ

I was singing "El Rancho Grande."

GROUCHO

Well, could you give us a little of—

GONZALEZ

Yes. *(Singing) Alla en el rancho grande* . . . Do you want it in English or Spanish?

GROUCHO

I don't know. What would you call that—what you just did?

GONZALEZ

"El Rancho Grande."

GROUCHO

I mean—would you call that English or Spanish?

GONZALEZ

Well, I think I call it English.

GROUCHO

Well, you do it in English then.

GONZALEZ

(Singing) Down on the big ranch, I have a beautifu-hul—

GROUCHO

No wonder you got the water.

79

GONZALEZ
I dance too.

GROUCHO
You do, huh? Well, could you do a little dance for us?

GONZALEZ
Sure! Why not?

GROUCHO
You come over here, Sally.

GONZALEZ
You want me to dance—what do you want me to dance? I dance Jarabe Tapatio. I dance La Bamba. I dance, you know.

GROUCHO
Well, do something you dance very well.

GONZALEZ
Okay. I dance Jarabe Tapatio. *(He does, singing at the same time)*

GROUCHO
Pedro, we could do a great act together. We could make a tour of vaudeville, you and I. What would we call our act? Two Hot Tamales?

GONZALEZ
No, we would call it Gonzalez Gonzalez and Marx.

GROUCHO
That's great billing. Two people in the act and I get third place.

Pedro Gonzalez Gonzalez and his partner, Sally Neidlinger, went on to qualify for the big question which, unfortunately, they didn't answer. During the quiz, Pedro kept looking up, trying to get the duck to come down. The audience broke up. Then, after having answered the third question, he asked if he could stop, because the money won so far would buy lots of beans and tortillas at home.

In retrospect, he was the most naturally funny contestant who ever appeared on our show. "This boy's the Mexican Jerry Lewis," I observed. The audience agreed, applauding for almost a minute.

PEDRO GONZALEZ GONZALEZ: After the show, the girl from the ski shop said to me, "Oh, my God! People went wild!"

When I came out, to tell the truth, I didn't know I was going to make people laugh. I just played myself. For it wasn't funny. Groucho started talking to me. And then he told me, "You already got two hundred dollars." And I say, "Is there any chance I can quit?" Because I meant it. Because two hundred dollars is a lot of money, you know. When he ask me how long I been married, I say nine years. So I just shake my head. You see, I suffer a lot when I was in Texas. I remember everything that happen to me. And it was true. It was me, you know. And all the people started laughing, and I thought, that's not funny. They ought to know what I went through with my wife. So I shake my head. Like I tell you, honest to God, it was the truth what happened to me, that show.

As soon as I finish, I take a couple of pictures with Groucho. All the people came running to me. Everybody try to hug me. I walk out, get onto the bus, and I went back. I had a little two-room house. Then one month later my boss call me. "Look what we got." So they show the show. I thought it was nothing.

So then they put it on the air. WOAI received about two hundred and fifty wires from all over the country. Truck drivers, they stop the truck to laugh, they were afraid to get into an accident.

So then everybody start looking for me. Nobody could find me. William Morris call the Walter O'Keefe people or Mr. Marx or his office. So William Morris flew over there. He went over there and knock at my door. I live in the Mexican neighborhood, you know. They never seen an American there. I thought it was a bill collector. He must find out that I got two hundred dollars in the bank. "Are you Gonzalez?" Yeah. "Do you live here?" Yeah. He say, "You know, you're one of the biggest things right now in Hollywood. And I want you to sign a contract. And here's a script. You're making a movie in two weeks." I say, "I can't make no movies. I don't read and write."

Pedro soon learned. He signed a personal contract with John Wayne, who said he's the greatest comedian since Chaplin, and that lasted for almost twenty years. He made several movie westerns and is now doing the Southwestern circuit, performing at rodeos and county fairs. His good works for the Mexican-American cause have been so appreciated that the city of San Antonio has named a municipal park after him.

And it all started with a scrawny kid coming on the show and stealing everyone's heart. Gonzalez Gonzalez was the most naturally funny contestant we ever had. His appearance was so talked about that it created increased momentum for us, and the show ended its season with its highest rating. The May, 1953, report of the American Research Bureau had our show running neck and neck with *I Love Lucy* and *Dragnet.*

Naturally, when you're doing a good job in one field, you're suddenly cast in another.

It was at about this time that I got a letter from some prominent Democrats asking me to run for governor of California. I was flattered, though not sure I was suited for the job.

I told them I was curious about one thing. "How much does a job like that pay?" I asked. They said I could get $25,000 a year. "Well," I told them, "I guess in your circle that's a pretty good salary. But I make that much in a couple of weeks. Thank you for your generous offer, but you'll have to get someone poorer than I am."

I was obliquely flattered to know that in the eyes of some I *looked* like a governor, just as Warren Harding *looked* like a President.

When Harding died, I was playing in Philadelphia at the Walnut Street Theatre. Word arrived, and it was my responsibility to pass the word to the audience. It was a dramatic scene. Rain was pelting the tin roof, and it was the fitting atmosphere for my somber message.

"Ladies and gentlemen," I started. "The President is dead." A gasp went up. Women started crying. "A great man is gone," I continued. "He will be greatly missed." Here I was, creating this tender scene for some schlemiel, whose place in history had already been set at a less than mediocre level.

Because I was doing a quiz show and seemed bright, Harry

Cohn at Columbia Pictures approached me about becoming a movie producer. I joined him at the studio for lunch one day.

He sat at a table with ten of his stooges. They all agreed with what Cohn said. At the end of lunch, I told him this was no place for me. Having seen my behavior during lunch, in which I tended to disagree with his every thought on general principles, he agreed it would be advisable if I continued in my present career. This I would do as soon as I returned from a tour of Europe.

DeSoto gave me two new cars every year. After stopping over in London, we would pick one up on the Continent, to use for touring.

We visited Parliament in London. The Guardsmen, with their stiff military bearing, and with an enforced taciturnity which would make Harpo livid with envy, went through the routine rigamarole for which they are famous. I was carrying an umbrella and, since a crowd had gathered, I started pantomiming their movements. The umbrella turned into a saber as I tried to break up one of the Guardsmen. I matched every one of his movements, but got no reaction. Finally as he stood at attention, I walked directly up to him and stared at the second button of his tunic, which was at my eye level. Out of the corner of his mouth, he said, "Copycat!"

We moved on to Paris. Though my father was a Frenchman, I didn't know any French at all, save for one of those perfunctory phrases a friend told me would cover all social situations.

"*Voulez-vous coucher avec moi?*" I asked several young ladies. I had my face slapped by a number of them.

We arrived in Germany. The last time I'd been there was as a boy of five. I'd returned to Dornum, my mother's birthplace, an international star. On the street one day, a little boy about eight years old came up and asked in German where I was from. I answered, "Chicago." With that, his eyes brightened. He made a revolver out of his hand, aimed it at me, and said, "Bang! Bang! Bang!"

On to Italy. Rome is a wonderful city. I was waiting for my

83

wife to finish dressing, cooling my heels on the street. I'd just lit a dollar cigar and was walking to the corner. Somebody bumped against me, knocking the cigar into the gutter. It was a dollar cigar. I wasn't going to let it lay there. So I reached down to pick it up, and said, "Jesus Christ!" I turned around and saw two priests standing next to me. And one of them had bumped against me. I was embarrassed. He reached into his coat, pulled out two cigars, and handed them to me. "Groucho, you just said the secret word!" The priests were from Cleveland.

I've always had funny experiences with priests. Once, I was at the Plaza Hotel and there was a priest in the elevator. He said, "Aren't you Groucho Marx?" And I said, "Yeah." He said, "My mother is crazy about that quiz show you do." I said to him, "I didn't know you fellows had mothers." The priest turned red. I tried to recover. "I always thought it was Immaculate Conception."

Then I was in Montreal. I was making a quick exit out of another elevator. A priest came up. "Groucho, I want to thank you for all the joy you've put into the world." I shook his hand. "Thank you, Father. And I want to thank you for all the joy you've taken out of it."

The priest laughed. "Could I use that next Sunday in my sermon?" "Yes, you can," I replied, "but you'll have to pay the William Morris office ten percent." Which I suppose was the first time a church had to pay a tithe instead of the other way around.

JERRY FIELDING: By 1953 I was very busy in this town. I had five radio shows and I was doing the Crescendo on Monday nights. Television was way in by then. We were roaring, and I was pretty much locked up at NBC.

I wasn't around all week; I didn't hang out in the office. Bob Dwan would call and tell me what category they wanted, and I'd write up the tunes and we'd rehearse them and play them. The show was so easy it was like stealing money. It wasn't even work. But it was a big mention every week. In those days everybody saw a hit show like that. You'll find people now who haven't seen All in the Family all over the place.

It would be nonsense for anybody who had any intelligence to say what happened was a surprise. I could see it coming. We were just hoping that somebody would wise up before it got out of hand.

When you get down to actual cases, assuming I was the most rabid security risk that you could dream of, what could I do to really upset anything playing fanfares on the Groucho Marx show? What kind of propaganda could I get across through that medium? And so, we all felt reasonably sanguine. Why would they bother with me?

There were two hundred and forty organizations on the Attorney General's un-American list, and I belonged to at least sixty of them. You wouldn't find anybody, except maybe the John Wayne group, that didn't belong to the Hollywood Writers Mobilization Committee during the war. I remember going to meetings when Artie Shaw and Johnny Green and Franz Waxman were running against each other for president. Groucho must have been involved in some of this. He would have had to be. He's that kind of guy.

In 1953 the House Un-American Activities Committee came out here. Gummo came in one day with an article in Walter Winchell's column and asked, "What is this all about?" The item said the committee had a subpoena out for me, and they were supposed to be looking for me. They didn't come to the right places, I guess, or didn't look hard enough. They frequently put these items out as a trial balloon, and this was supposed to scare you, and then you were supposed to go running to them to name a whole bunch of people. Gummo was very upset. Groucho pooh-poohed the whole thing.

The committee left town and everybody forgot about it. Then the subcommittee came back. It was just before Thanksgiving that they hung the thing on me.

I got the subpoena at the show. They waltzed in when I was getting ready to go on the air and they laid this thing on me. So I took the thing into my hand and walked into Groucho's dressing room. I waved it in his face and said, "I quit. I'm saving you the trouble. Get yourself another fellow." He said he wouldn't have that. He would not sit still for a political firing.

Although NBC wasn't nearly as rabid about it or as infected with it as CBS—they had special lists in drawers over there—the network said they had a big investment in me and they didn't need that kind of trouble. They had a general distaste for the whole thing.

They pinned me in a corner and asked, "What are you going to do?" I said, "I'm going to go in there and be an unfriendly witness. I'm not

85

going to cooperate with these people because I have nothing to tell them that I feel is in any way criminal. And I will not just wreck a lot of people to save my neck."

This very nice vice-president at NBC said I was going to go in there and come out smelling like a rose.

The only thing I could think of that he might understand was to say something that I probably had no right to say. I knew where Groucho's sentiment was and how he felt about certain things. I said, "What do I say when they ask me about Groucho? It's fine if they knock me off. What do I mean? But if any dirt gets spilled on him, it's going to cost you a lot of money, and I'm not going to be the guy that's going to spill any dirt on him."

Well, he turned his whole tune around immediately. The NBC vice-president suddenly understood what the implications were and how many people were being named.

We went in on a hearing on Wednesday morning, and of course I did what I said I would do. I took the Fifth Amendment. As was the case in all Congressional hearings of this kind, you don't have any of the privileges of Anglo-Saxon jurisprudence that you have in court. It's not a trial. There is no accusation, and under the rules of the committee you either testify or you don't. But you can only do it under the Fifth Amendment.

The only way that would stick in court was to refuse to discuss anything other than your name and address. Nothing about your past. You could talk about what you were doing now, because they weren't investigating what you were doing now. But anything regarding your past, you couldn't discuss at all. I mean any of it, because you could not be selective about the questions you chose to answer. For example, if they wanted to ask, "Were you a member of the American Nazi Party?" I would have said no. I would have then been stuck to answer every question about everybody in every other organization they asked me about, because I'd answered one question in the area. One Congressman, just before he excused me, asked, "Are you a member of the Communist party?" I said no. He said, "Were you a member of the Communist party when you came into this room thirty-five minutes ago?" I said, "I refuse to answer the question." He said, "Five minutes ago?" Again I refused to answer the question. So that's all that went into the paper. I was on the front page of the late afternoon edition, and it reported that I wasn't a Communist, but I wouldn't say whether I was one five minutes ago.

Bob Dwan is the sweetest man in the world. He was the only one who

86

appeared to be bleeding at the pores over this whole thing. He called on a Tuesday and said, "Well, you know, Groucho doesn't want to fire you or anything like that. But we feel maybe it's a little tender at the moment, and we have a live audience. Maybe you ought not to come tomorrow night."

I said, "I'll get someone to cover for me." So I got Lynn Murray. Well, Lynn Murray had written a preface to a People's Songbook *that Pete Seeger had put out in 1932. When they found out he was on the show, some grocer from Syracuse or somebody came out with that fact in his paper, and said the guy that went on in my place had also been tainted, and the whole program must be littered with Commies.*

After that, I couldn't get Bob on the phone, I couldn't get Groucho, I couldn't get my agent, I couldn't get NBC. It was as though I didn't exist. I never saw any of them again. They never even bothered to fire me. It was just as if I'd turned to gas. I must say I began to burn.

By putting me on that show, there's no question that Groucho did something for me. He made it possible for me to become enough of a household word to be able to get a lot of other work. But I did get angry, because I felt that he didn't make enough of an effort to stop this thing. I felt, being who he was, that he was strong enough to take a stand right then and there. But he didn't do it. Somehow he got frightened off. I think the people with all the money in this talked him out of it. I took a burn at him, and I didn't want to talk to him.

The name of the self-righteous supermarket owner, lest we forget, was Laurence Johnson. I let myself be fooled, but not for long. Sadly, the damage was already done. That I bowed to sponsors' demands is one of the greatest regrets of my life.

JOHN GUEDEL: It was an unfair thing, and the whole atmosphere of the time. Big business was scared to death of this Communist thing and they just didn't want to take any chances. All of the companies that were sponsors at that time were disassociating themselves from anybody with leftist tendencies. It was a sort of rule of thumb. They were trying to sell their product to everybody and they were afraid what the public would think. They'd boycott their products. But this wasn't a decision exclusive to us, and I don't think the networks had a lot to do with it, because at that time networks were pretty much controlled by sponsors—the half-hour shows were. Nowadays expenses are so high that very few shows are. The sponsor ordered us to do it. We could have been Joan of Arcs ourselves, but unfortunately we said, "Okay, if you insist." Well, Jerry Fielding was a great talent and fortunately he came through and probably did a hell of a lot better.

JERRY FIELDING: I arranged one thing with Dwan. I asked him not to fire anybody in the band. I will say that the boys stayed, and that was about as good as anybody got. After that, the blacklist was on, but I've never been out of a job. I went on the road with a band right away, and wound up in Las Vegas.

JACK MEAKIN: They evidently had two or three names in the hat. When Bob Dwan saw my name, he said, "Why didn't I think of him myself?" We'd worked together at NBC in San Francisco. It took awhile for me to be told I had the job. What was happening, I guess, was that they were checking my background. They had to get a clearance on me.

I came on just before Christmas of 1953. We had twelve people in the band, including myself. When Jerry had it there was no piano. I went on, and being a piano player, I filled in on the piano. That made it a bit easier, because when they had to do so many ad lib things—like if somebody was singing—I could start playing the piano and the rest of the fellows would follow me.

The show always used "Captain Spaulding" as a basic opening theme. Jerry had another tune that went with it. Then I went on and wrote another theme. It was called "Groucho and the Wolf." It was nothing to do with Tchaikovsky, or "Peter and the Wolf." It was just the title to the beat arrangement, and I thought it was sort of funny.

Time and again it was brought home to me that we should treat the quiz portion with a reasonable amount of seriousness. Money, to the contestants, was nothing to joke about. One week I'd opened the program with, "Here we are again with a chance for each of our couples to win two thousand dollars, and there's even a chance somebody might leave here tonight with ten thousand dollars. But if he does, we'll slug him outside." It wasn't one of our biggest laughs.

ROBERT DWAN: We rarely got letters of protest over anything Groucho said to the contestants. The only contestant I think that we got any kind of reaction from, and it was mainly from the network, was with Norman Carroll, the ringmaster for the circus. It wasn't because it was particularly censorable. Norman Carroll was a lovely man, and he came on and simply started talking. He was a very shrewd guy and wise in show business ways. He started trying to tell Groucho how he was washing his car on a Sunday afternoon. Groucho never let him finish the story. Norman was enjoying it tremendously. It was his task to try to tell the story of how he washed the car. I don't think the thing had any payoff particularly. Groucho just kept interrupting him and asking him all kinds of different tangential questions. Carroll never got around to finishing the story. We thought it was hilarious. The studio audience was enjoying it. Norman was enjoying it. Groucho was having a lovely time. But we got lots of letters from people about not letting that nice man finish his story, and that's the only program I know that the network asked us not to repeat in the summer. That's the only time, as far as I know, that we got letters from people, because there was no way anything really objectionable was ever going to sneak into that thing, unless I just didn't realize it.

(We should have had Norman Carroll on again and let him complete the story. And we will, as soon as I start my new quiz series. Maybe this time I'll be the one in the more sympathetic light.)

There were other times, if the thing didn't work with the contestants, we'd at least have the prepared jokes for Groucho to read. We'd use them and then go into the quiz, and a lot of times we damn near didn't ask them anything when the final version was shown. That's when people began to think Groucho was rude and unfeeling about people. He'd get somebody up there who looked fascinating going in, and it turns out he didn't have a damned thing to talk about, or their personalities were wrong and it didn't work.

(Occasionally, a contestant was so unsympathetic, with no help from me, that I would have to get to the quiz as soon as possible. I wouldn't let him hang himself . . . or me.)

HOWARD HARRIS: If the guests were disappointing, Groucho didn't give them as long. He'd drop the interview and get to the game. There was only one fail-safe line: "Now it's time to play You Bet Your Life."

Most of the contestants expected to be insulted by Groucho. They'd all seen the show. They knew his character and they went along with the gag. If they weren't insulted they were insulted.

89

ROBERT DWAN: I was usually standing right out of camera range, and I'd get a feeling of what was happening most of the time whenever the contestant said something. The studio audience knew what Groucho was going to respond. Then he either fulfilled that expectation by saying what they thought he was going to say—and then they laughed—or he would say something else which they didn't expect him to say at all, and that was even better. That was the interaction with the studio audience. They were always guessing and anticipating. What made it funny was whether Groucho fulfilled the anticipation or not.

A lot of times, through editing, I made him appear rude to the people. He interrupted them, didn't let them finish. He propably did let them finish, but it wasn't as funny.

(Bob Dwan is a man of enormous taste, and he largely established the classy level of the show. Even if I'd wanted to, he wouldn't let me stoop to the gutter. But if he made me appear to be rude through his editing, then I'm afraid it was a case of bad editing. I always kidded the contestants. I was never rude, and I find it surprising at this late date that so many of my associates on the show still think otherwise.)

There was no formula as such for the show. It's so intuitive. In looking at them today, I realize there had to be a foundation. What I did find out is that being interesting is not enough . . . not in a half-hour format. It has to be funny.

Apparently, the format that evolved for *You Bet Your Life* contained innately humorous elements, for it was copied for a great many of my guest appearances on other shows.

I'd previously re-created it at a Writer's Guild dinner, with Norman Krasna and Jerry Wald playing the contestants. I'd also done it as a guest on Jack Benny's show, with Jack playing a contestant, disguised in a wig, because he wanted to win the grand prize of $2,500. (He was tripped up on the big question: What is Jack Benny's real age?)

The most ambitious production, however, took place on March 28, 1954, when General Foods bought out the prime time of all three television networks to mount a salute to Richard Rodgers and Oscar Hammerstein. Mary Martin was mistress of ceremonies, and the stars appearing included Ezio Pinza, Yul Brynner, Rosemary Clooney, Tony Martin, Jack Benny, and Edgar Bergen.

Our routine, written by Bernie, Bob, and me, went like this:

(Scene: Groucho is sitting on his stool beside his stand . . . The announcer at one of the two contestant mikes . . . The set a duplicate of that used on You Bet Your Life.)

GROUCHO: Well, here I am again with two dollars and seventy-five cents for one of our couples. I haven't got my sponsor with me and I'm using my own money, so that's as high as I intend to go. And just to be sure that nobody wins anything, the secret word tonight is: "Antidisestablishmentarianism." Okay, let's have the first couple.

ANNCR: We asked if there was anybody in the audience with anything interesting to say. We didn't find anybody, so for want of something better we selected these two men from the audience. And here they are—a Mr. Rodgers and a Mr. Hammerstein. Gentlemen, meet Groucho Marx.

(Anncr. exits, they enter . . . Applause)

GROUCHO: Welcome to *You Bet Your Life.* Say the secret word and I'll cut my throat from ear to ear. It's a common word, something you find around the house.

HAMMER: Is it "Antidisestablishmentarianism?"

GROUCHO: No, I'm sorry. I heard somebody whisper that from the audience. All right, let's get on with it. Now let's see. Who are you two again? *(Looks at name card on stand).* Say, you're pretty famous! Every kid in the country knows *you! Roy Rogers!* King of the Cowboys! Then this must be Trigger, eh?

RODGERS: No, that's Hammerstein.

GROUCHO: Odd name for a horse. Odd name even for a man! Honestly now, Roy—wouldn't you rather kiss a girl occasionally instead of the horse all the time?

ROGERS: Sorry, I'm not *Roy* Rogers . . . Harpo!

GROUCHO: Harpo! How would you like it if I came down to

your studio and poured glue in your piano? And you're Oscar Hammerstein, eh? Well, it's a great honor to have you here. (Shake hands) You're the fellow that opened the Manhattan Opera House in 1906.

HAMMER: No, Mr. Marx. You've got me and my grandfather confused.

GROUCHO: That's not true—I've never had your grandfather confused. Your grand*mother* may have had him confused, but I never did.

HAMMER: What I meant was, you're thinking of my grandfather.

GROUCHO: You're wrong again. Actually, I was thinking of Marilyn Monroe. But if your grandfather was the famous Oscar Hammerstein, who are you?

HAMMER: I'm Oscar Hammerstein the Second.

GROUCHO: The second! Well, I guess when you're doing a benefit, you have to put up with seconds. Well, let's find out something about you two. What sort of work do you do, Mr. —(*Looks at card again*)—Hammerlock?

HAMMER: It's Hammerstein. I'm a famous song writer.

GROUCHO: A song writer! Well, what are you doing up here with this cowboy?

HAMMER: He's a famous song writer too.

GROUCHO: You certainly had me fooled. I would have guessed you were a couple of chiropractors. Have you written anything that anybody's ever heard of?

RODGERS: Well, we wrote *Oklahoma!, Carousel, South Pacific, The King and I, Me and Juliet,* and some other things.

GROUCHO: Wait a minute. Didn't you fellows write a thing called *Allegro?* Now you don't have to answer that. If you want to, you can stand on the Fifth Amendment. Let me put it this way: Have you ever had a real song hit . . . like "Ricochet Romance" or "Cow Cow Boogie"?

RODGERS: We had one song that did pretty well. It's called "Some Enchanted Evening." It sold a couple of million records.

92

GROUCHO: Now just a moment. I happen to know something about the record business, and there must be some reason for a sale like that. Come clean now—what was on the other side of "Some Enchanted Evening"?

RODGERS: I forget. Oscar, what *was* on the other side of it?

HAMMER: I'm not sure. I think it was "There Is Nothing Like a Dame."

GROUCHO: Well, that accounts for it. If you're gonna drag sex into it, you can sell anything! Now that you mention it, I have heard "Some Enchanted Evening." So you're the fellows who wrote it, eh? Well, it's a darn nice little tune. By the way, I wish you'd explain something to me. How did you ever happen to hit on the idea of writing it in an Italian dialect? Now, is this the extent of your song hits?

HAMMER: No, we wrote one about you—"Surly with the Fringe on Top"!

GROUCHO: Well, enough of this antidisestablishmentarianism. I can work a word into the conversation too, you know. I knew who you were all the time. I was just pretending not to know how much magic you've given to the theater. You know, there's a question I always ask on my show, and I'm sure it will be of interest to this audience. How did you two happen to get married? I mean, what happened the very first time you met Oscar, Dick? Do you remember?

RODGERS: Well, the very first time, I was only twelve years old and Oscar was nineteen and a real big man on the Columbia University campus. It was a big moment for a kid like me. It was like meeting Eisenhower.

GROUCHO: Why was that? Did he have a golf club in his hand? I have another question I'm sure you're often asked. Oscar, what would you say is the secret of this blending of two great talents? How is it you work so perfectly together?

HAMMER: (*He gives his opinions of Rodgers' music*)

GROUCHO: Dick, how would you explain it?

RODGERS: (*Explains how Hammerstein's lyrics are real poetry—simple, honest, etc. They demand original music. Example, line: "Corn is as high as an elephant's eye," etc.*)

GROUCHO: Well, it's been very informative talking to you two. I haven't learned anything, but I'm sure you haven't either. Now you're going to play *You Bet Your Life*. We start you off with ten dollars.

HAMMER: Just a moment. On your show you start them off with a hundred dollars.

GROUCHO: When I want your opinion, I'll ask for it. Okay, I'll start you off with a hundred dollars. But I warn you, you'll know you've been in a battle. Okay, let's go. You selected General Information. Now here's your first question. Ready? The orchestra will play a well-known selection. You identify it. Play, Leopold.

OBOE: (*Plays one short but loud "beeeep"*)

GROUCHO: All right. What was that? And please, no help from the audience!

RODGERS: That was the first oboe's fifth note in the counterpoint of the second coda from the third act of *Allegro*.

GROUCHO: I didn't think the show ran long enough for you to remember it. Okay. You've got a hundred dollars. Now for your second question. (*To audience*) They're pretty cocky, but wait'll they get a load of this next one. Ready? "If you had five cubic meters of concrete, how many cubic *feet* of concrete would you have? And I want you to do it using only Roman numerals. Quickly now.

HAMMER: Roman numerals? (*Figures aloud*) Let's see . . . V times XXX-point-MMCLXXV equals CLXXVI-point-V, with a line over it, DCCXV.

GROUCHO: That was a pretty sneaky answer. Only a sneak would know a thing like that. However, you haven't trapped the old quizmaster yet. Here's your third question: "What was the whale oil production of Norway in 1951?"

HAMMER: Long tons or short tons?

94

GROUCHO: I'll accept long tons, because I'm a friendly old quizmaster.

HAMMER: That would be one hundred seventy thousand five hundred forty-two tons.

GROUCHO: Very good, Oscar. You're a fine student. Now you stay after school and I'll flog you to a jelly. Well, now you've got three hundred dollars. This is ridiculous. This kind of money will never do you any good, so I'll keep it myself. However, the next question I'll make worth your while. Get it right and I'll do something people have been pleading with me to do for fifteen years. That is, return to the New York theater. I've turned hundreds of offers down the last fifteen years, but if you get this last question right, I'll consent to star in your next Broadway show.

(R & H look at each other questioningly)

GROUCHO: Ready? Gimme the title of this song. Play, Dmitri.

ORCH: *(Title phrase of* "Some Enchanted Evening" . . . *R & H huddle)*

GROUCHO: All right, what's the answer you two have decided upon?

RODGERS: "My Old Kentucky Home."

GROUCHO: That's right! It's not exactly right, but beggars can't be choosers. Now when do we start rehearsals?

(R & H huddle, nod, frown)

HAMMER: Mr. Marx, there's nothing personal in this, but if this is what's facing us, we've decided to quit show business.

GROUCHO: Well, thanks and good luck from the more than three thousand Rescue Missions all over America!

ROBERT DWAN: We'd see in the paper somebody who set some sort of goofy record or had a lot of kids or something like that, or Bernie would decide that, "Gee, it would be fun to have a tree surgeon." And so we'd go and talk to a bunch of tree surgeons until we found one that looked like he had some brains and had some kind of personality. We'd also have the people that come in and say, "I'd like to be on the show," and sit down and talk to them and found out if they really had any-thing to say. That's the prime preparation. Anybody that got up there had something to talk about.

MARION POLLOCK: My principal job in recruiting contestants was to read the papers and look for human interest stories. I would also call very famous people and persuade them to go on. John Charles Thomas was one. I talked him into it. Another was Richard Armour, the humorist. There was resistance among celebrities. Nobody wanted to match wits with Groucho, with the chance his public image would be damaged. A woman has certain ways to get them on where a man can't. She can smile amiably. I was able to persuade them.

Sometimes, after the program, the contestants would walk off the stage. I would be cringing inside about the caustic things Groucho had said to them. Here I'd talked them into going on, and had promised to protect them. They'd invariably say, "It wasn't so bad." They loved the experience.

BERNIE SMITH: Of the two thousand five hundred contestants that went through, I remember only one who didn't get on the air. He was an East Indian, such a nice, quiet, little man. But he didn't project.

We had several cases where we couldn't repeat the shows during the summer. One was a law student in his senior year. Though he'd signed the release, he asked us not to air his show again. "By that time I'll have my license," he said, "and it's unethical for a lawyer to get pub-licity."

In other cases, the contestants died shortly after their appearances. Two of them were murdered: a German war bride and a girl found dead in an actor's swimming pool.

In a couple of other instances I decided not to repeat the shows on which a couple of elected officials were on. I almost did it as a civic duty. Why should I let total jerks reflect on their hometowns, even if they are a city councilman and a judge?

Shortly after we'd gone on radio, Doc Tyler had come on the show as part of the program staff. He wrote good jokes, and I suppose it's an indictment of our society that he should make more money as a joke writer than as one of the coun-try's leading authorities on fertility. He left the show at the end of our fourth television season to return to the field of medicine.

HOWARD HARRIS: I was on the program staff for the last seven years. When I came on the formula was already established. The only difference I remember is that at the beginning there was the façade of getting people out of the audience. This was set up and it looked phony, so it was eliminated.

I've been a comedy writer for many years, and all during the time I was on the show there was always the fantasy that no writers are connected with it. Most people think the show was one hundred percent ad lib. It was nevertheless the most spontaneous show on the air, but the contestants had to know what to feed Groucho.

People on the show were screened. They were interviewed thoroughly. Then they were teamed up with another person, and it was then put together.

Groucho would then get into the act, making his comments and ad libs. Then the final show was done. The comments at the script conference were saved. They might or might not be utilized on the show.

We never knew what he would say. Overall he had a high average of ad libs. There were an incredible number of laughs per half hour. We didn't use any canned-laughter machine.

From the time I first interviewed a person until I actually saw him on the screen, it might take three months. Consequently I can't remember my funny lines. Sometimes, though, I'd see them flash across the screen. One of them was when the girl told Groucho, "I'm waiting for Mr. Right." He answered, "Orville or Wilbur?"

JERRY FIELDING: Groucho came up to Las Vegas a couple of times and would sit very close to us. I wouldn't speak to him. I'm sure that hurt him, and that he felt bad about what happened.

MARION POLLOCK: Each time we did the show I was there. My job was to circulate among the guests, to keep them relaxed and calm. I led them on stage. I had to time it so they wouldn't hear the secret word, then I led them on with a smile.

BERNIE SMITH: The show was absolutely spontaneous. Groucho never saw the people in advance. He really didn't know for sure what they were going to say. And he was caught by surprise on almost every-

thing. *The contestants didn't know what Groucho was going to say. All they knew was what they were going to say, which was in their own words. We never made anything up, so the people were alive all the time.*

Groucho didn't want to get that closely involved in the preparation. He wanted to be fresh when he went out there. We had a pretty good idea, but time after time Groucho would come out there, and be wild, and we had no idea what was happening. That's when we had the great shows.

When he was at his peak you could never write for this man. He was much better than any writer could ever be.

JACK MEAKIN: *There were two of us who listened for the secret word. Number one on the totem pole was the trumpet player. That was part of his job, and, as I recall, he got paid a little over scale to be the duck listener. Morey Harris sat throughout the show just listening for the word. The moment he heard it, boom! I was responsible for backing him up, so I sat and also listened for it. But, of course, I'm a funloving rover and I was laughing at the show most of the time. Then if I missed it, next in line was Bob Dwan. If we were all sitting there sound asleep, then Bob would start waving like crazy and throwing the cue and finally we would play the thing. But this didn't happen very often.*

I also had a straight-ahead view of the wheel, and I could see the people. You could tell whether it was going to be a fast spin or a slow spin. When the women did it, they usually did it perfunctorily, and it would be a slow spin. I knew then what I had to do. We had this thing, bar by bar, that went down one tone each time. At the end of each one of those bars was a chord where we could stop.

GEORGE FENNEMAN: *Either the lady was going to pick me up or there would be guys with whips, or I'd shortly be flying around the stage.*

Like with the strong woman. She was a very good looking woman, but very strong. Groucho said, "Pick up Fenneman." And she picked me up around the knees. This woman had my knees in her bosom, in front of all these people and she wouldn't put me down. Here you are, a grown man with children at home, and this woman is holding you in the air.

Or the guys with the whips . . . twins. I had just come out of the

98

hospital with a double hernia operation. I was still a little bent over, you know, and every time I moved I could feel it. I still had the stitches. And I had to stand there while they flicked things out of my mouth or whatever.

Of course, the actuality was sometimes an anticlimax. One week we had a woman on the show with fifty cats. And wouldn't you know, I'm allergic to cats. And backstage there were fifty cages for these cats. I told the producers that if I got hair near my face I would cry and sneeze. So I worried all night and then nothing happened. When I was called out, luckily, I just had to bring the cages out.

BERNIE SMITH: Nobody bothered us much about what we put on the show. We had no censorable material, and the networks had no reason to complain about plugs or payola because we were more sensitive about them than the networks.

There were only two instances where we had some difficulty with the sponsor. The ad agency made John Anson Ford, the son of a Los Angeles supervisor, change his name because they said we couldn't have a Ford on a DeSoto show.

Another thing that made me mad: they got wind that I'd paired a white girl with a black man. It wasn't a conceivable romantic thing. The agency said that DeSoto dealers would revolt. I paired them anyway and there was a big flap about it.

We opened our fifth season on NBC with an appearance of one of our most distinguished guests, General Omar Bradley, who was paired with a WAC.

He is a great man, with the ability to laugh at himself. And he endeared himself to the audience when he was forced to concede that he had never won a Good Conduct Medal.

ROBERT DWAN: There were several attempts to imitate the show with very good comics such as Fred Allen, Herb Shriner, and Edgar Bergen. But all tried to do it live. They were bound by the half hour and couldn't take a chance that something funny would happen. They all fed funny things for people to say. We didn't have to do it because we were working a longer time and could let it go. The ability to edit was a very important thing. If it wasn't funny at all, it wasn't used. We gave Groucho the crutches to lean on.

> *No one else did this extravagant thing of having eight cameras go-
> ing as long as we wanted to go. We never stopped. Today we would
> have to run four videotape cameras and four tape recorders to get the
> same effect.*

There was indeed one show that was mounted in an equally extravagant manner. One of our staff defected to go over
to CBS. He would be working on *Do You Trust Your Wife?*,
starring Edgar Bergen, which began broadcasting in January, 1955.

EDGAR BERGEN: When we started Do You Trust Your
Wife? *we more or less duplicated the system of eight or nine cameras
that Groucho was using. He has reason not to like me for that, I guess,
but it wasn't my doing. It was just the technique that was being used.*

*We got on in New York from ten to eleven, which was too late. We
lost all the old people and the young people. Out here we got on at eight,
from west of Denver, so we were always in the first five, and in the last
two months we were Number One on the West Coast.*

*The show ran for two years. We went on in January, and we went
off two years later in January, because one sponsor dropped out. We
thought we had another sponsor set, and then he reneged. And that's no
time to start a show, you know. You just have to replace another show,
so that was unfortunate. But once it's off the air, it's almost a dead
thing.*

*JERRY FIELDING: In 1955 the Treasury Department came
through Las Vegas and they wanted to put a band on the air to sell
bonds. They asked me to do it. I said, "I'm not going to do it. I can't
get a passport. I'm being followed by the FBI everywhere I go. I'm not
going to even risk another security check."*

*The head of the casino came to me and said, "What in the hell is this
bullshit? You're going to do it."*

*I did it. I was on for thirty-nine weeks with the United States Gov-
ernment for a sponsor. I couldn't work for Colgate or any network, you
see, but I could work for them. It didn't make any sense.*

*And we went on tour, and we played every military installation in
the area. We played places where nobody could go.*

*By then the McCarthy hearings were on, and it was beginning to
fall apart.*

Perspective was returning to the American conscience, and the scattershot accusations abated somewhat. It was scant consolation that, while some careers were interrupted, few of them were totally ruined.

Another form of hysteria, however, would soon plague those of us in television. The big-money quiz shows. Edgar Bergen's show, which started broadcasting at virtually the same time as *The $64,000 Question,* was at a disadvantage. Edgar was offering great entertainment at a time when the American public was at its most materialistic, and living vicariously through the acquisition of great sums of money by others. Even so, his show was a big hit. I watched it on many a Sunday night.

MARION POLLOCK: I knew darn well The $64,000 Question *was crooked because we had one of their contestants first on our show. When I read he was winning all that money on the other show, I knew something was wrong. He was a cute guy, but not all that bright.*

In a very short time, *The $64,000 Question* was at the top of the ratings, and it began spawning imitators. We stayed in the Top Ten, but we had to work a lot harder to do so.

BERNIE SMITH: There were three basic elements that made our show unique, that made it successful. One, we had the incomparable Groucho, who was capable of anything. Two, we had great contestants. And three, we had good people who did the basic interviews to get out the information. Sometimes they'd have to dig for hours to find one line. Now if all three of those elements worked and the audience was good, if Groucho was really feeling good and liked the people, and if the planning of the show in advance was right, we had a great show. To have a good show we had to have two out of those three elements working. If we only had one, then we were in trouble.

Here's where we had our escape hatch. The recording. This gave Groucho all the latitude he needed. If he liked somebody, if he was on to something hot or interesting, he would pursue it just as long as he wanted until something happened. And he's a bulldog. If he thinks there's a joke there, he will go on with it. There'll be miles of film going all over the floor. But sooner or later he'll get the laugh. What wound up on the air was the distillation of all these elements through the editing of all that film. Editing was kind of like writing the show after the fact.

If there was ever any doubt that our audience was still with us it was removed at about this time when a potato farmer came on as a contestant.

"Does anyone still know how to make that good old fashioned German potato salad?" I asked him. *Kartoffel Salat.* It brought back childhood memories. I don't recall his reply, but I do remember the carloads of potato salad that descended upon us after the show was aired, as well as the hundreds of recipes.

I ran into Tennessee Ernie Ford at NBC.

"I hear you have a lot of potato salad," he said.

"Sixteen tons," I replied.

He chuckled. "Another day older and deeper in debt."

The rest is history.

The A. C. Nielsen ratings showed that we had a significant drop in viewers just as the big-money quiz shows came on. In January of 1955 we were reaching 13,630,000 homes, and 43.7 percent of TV homes were tuned to the program during the average minute. These figures dipped in January of 1956 to 12,500,000 and 35.6 percent of TV homes tuned per average minute.

It was during the calendar year of 1956 that the greatest number of our most memorable guests appeared on *You Bet Your Life.*

They were led off on February 2 with the appearance of a suburban housewife.

HY FREEDMAN: I wrote thousands of lines over the years. The trick wasn't so much writing the funny line. It was getting the interview so that it came out funny. The funniest contestant was Gonzalez Gonzalez, but the best one was Esther Bradley.

We'd never done a whole show with just one set of contestants, though I'd suggested it a number of times. She came along, and within a couple of minutes I knew she was a real winner. I just steered her

102

along. Her answers were really great. This was to be the classic show against which we measured all the others. You really didn't write it. It was all in the interview.

I went to Bernie and said, "You have to let her go the whole show." She could have done another whole show on her marriage. It was replete with the same things.

ROBERT DWAN: Groucho knew the questions to ask the contestants. He'd know this one has got a funny story about how he met his wife, and that one has a funny occupation. With Esther Bradley, and what she did for a living, all you needed was, "And then what did you do?" And, "How long did you keep the job?" and, "What did you do after that?" He could have asked her about how many children she had and where she went to school, but he didn't. We knew that Esther had some funny things to say about jobs she'd goofed up. Now we didn't have any idea about how funny it was going to play, and there weren't any particular jokes. There are some mild ones there.

Esther Bradley gave the impression that she was so stupid that she didn't have enough sense to find the studio by herself. We should all be so stupid. Esther was simply wonderful. Her delivery was droll and self-mocking. She was like a highly trained comedienne in the Minnie Pearl tradition.

She talked of Matamoros, Pennsylvania, her birthplace, and the misadventures that plagued her ever since she was a child. Her first job was in a lipstick factory, but that didn't last long.

"Why not?" I asked.

"The things they asked you to do, you know," she replied.

"Well, what did they ask you to do?"

"Work."

I asked her to clarify that.

"I had to work on a conveyor belt. I had to put the little lipstick on the pegs."

But it didn't work out for her. She had a cold, and what with dabbing at her nose with Kleenex, she made a botch of the assembly line. She was transferred to another department, where Esther claimed she was similarly ineffectual.

After she put the lipstick factory out of business she moved on to another job.

"And what was it?"

"I went to work," she responded, "for the government."

Esther worked in Death Claims and Retirements, but she had to leave the job when she broke her ankle.

"Where do you work now?" I asked.

"I work at Lockheed," she said. "They make planes."

"Folks," I said, "next time take the train."

Our discussion touched briefly on her husband.

"I'd like to meet him," I told her. "When are the visiting hours?"

Esther took it all with great aplomb. The program nearly conducted itself. She was a marvel.

When it came time for the quiz, Esther said, "I can't answer those questions because I don't know anything about— much."

"Would you like someone to fill in?" I asked.

"Yes, somebody with brains."

I turned to the audience. "Is there somebody out there who would like to fill in for Esther? How about a three-year-old boy?"

A serviceman came up from the audience and answered the questions with Esther's partner, Joe Egbert.

Esther went on to have a mildly successful career as a country-western singer and comedienne, but she never could have been as brilliant and original as she was when the national audience first saw her on our show.

In September another budding entertainer appeared on the show. His name was Kuldip Rae Singh, a handsome young Pakistani attending medical school in the United States. He confided his dilemma, for he had a romantic baritone singing voice, and wondered if he should pursue a career in show business. After he sang "A Woman in Love" to his teen-age partner there wasn't any doubt.

BERNIE SMITH: Kuldip created a greater reaction than any oth-

104

er contestant. He wandered into our office one day. Marion Pollock and Eddie Mills really had to sell me on this kid, because I didn't like the idea of him at all. Marion and Eddie both said, "You've got to. He's a good-looking kid, he's got a great voice, and he's got a good personality." Finally I gave in. After we did the show and Dwan saw the film, he called me and said, "That kid should get an agent, because he's going to be a sensation." I wasn't interested in getting him an agent or doing anything for him other than to protect him from the wolves. Kuldip had gone to Puerto Rico, where his family was, after he appeared on the show. He didn't tell me he was going down there. The day after the show was aired all hell broke loose. Eddie Mills' phone was ringing off the hook. The musical director of a record company called and insulted me all over the place because I couldn't deliver Kuldip right now. Every studio in town wanted him. He was an overnight sensation. I'd told him, "Whatever you do, don't sign with anybody, don't do anything, just in case you're a success, until you talk to me." He remembered that. Well, Ben Bard, who was head of the acting school for Twentieth Century Fox, called. He talked to Eleanor Rowan, the show's secretary. She didn't know that I was protecting Kuldip so she said, "We don't know where he is. All we know is that he's with his family in Puerto Rico." That's all the clue that Bard had. He went down to Puerto Rico and literally kidnapped Kuldip. He took him to a hotel in New York so that he couldn't communicate with anybody, and he did his best to get him to sign a studio contract. Fortunately Kuldip held out. He finally came back, and I went to meet him at the plane. And there's Ben Bard coming off the plane with him. Kuldip saw me and came over. I said, "Look, get rid of all these guys. I have to talk to you."

One of my old friends was a vice-president at MCA, and I talked them into signing him. But Kuldip was a dreamer. He wasn't a practical kid at all. He got tons of fan mail. MCA would call him and they'd say, "Come on, Kuldip, you have to go over to Columbia and cut a record." That's the last they'd hear from Kuldip. He'd stay in his room reading his fan mail. Finally MCA said to hell with it. He just threw away a great career. He just drifted out of sight.

At that same time, while Kuldip Singh was forfeiting a career for which he had no great dedication, another newcomer to show business was giving it her all.

She was a housewife approaching middle age, and George

Fenneman recommended that she come on the show as a contestant.

PHYLLIS DILLER: At the time I had nobody but myself working for me, and really it was just word of mouth, people like George Fenneman. Lots of Hollywood people came up regularly to the Purple Onion in San Francisco. Out of that place during that era came the Smothers Brothers, the Kingston Trio, Randy Sparks, Rod McKuen, Jim Nabors, Ronnie Schell, myself. It was a hotbed of talent.

My second job was down in Los Angeles. It's a place now called The Losers, but originally it was John Walsh's 881 Club. It was very small, posh, chic, an inside-show-biz-type place. Through a glass there was a bar, which was entirely gay, and then a very small showroom peopled mostly by stars.

I happened to be in Hollywood one whole month. This was late in 1956. Before I went on the show, there were in-depth, psychological interviews . . . long interviews just to become a contestant. They do less questioning before a serious operation.

There were no questions that put me off. None have ever put me off in my whole lifetime. I have answers I probably will never have a chance to use. I'll never forget. Everyone was a different interviewer . . . lots of questions about past history.

Part of those long hours must have had something to do with the show, deciding what I was going to do, and how I was going to work things out. I was brought on as a housewife contestant, which was true. At that time I was still living with my entire family. I was holed up in a motel with four of the kids. I took care of them during the day and went down to the Walsh place at night to work.

In that particular appearance I was wearing the first sack dress on television. It had never been worn before. You know how they cite new shapes and styles—female toggery—and I bought it especially for the show. Because I didn't have any clothes. I was new in the business and broke, and this was to be my first television appearance.

The contestant with me was a physicist. Brilliant man, at a laboratory outside L.A. I saw him recently. It was like old home week.

I did a little piece of an airline routine. I can't remember how it went, not after nineteen years, because I must have dropped it fifteen years ago. I only did a teensy bit of it.

Here, for poserity, is the first routine Phyllis did on television:

106

"Mr. Marx was talking about his psychiatrist. Well, I decided I'd better be well-adjusted before I went into such a shaky business. So I decided I should be analyzed, and I went to this analyst. He helped me a great deal. In fact, I'm so much better now that I get to sit up.

"He cured me of a lot of things that were making me insecure. Well, like I used to be freckled. He cured me of that. (*Holds up bare arm*) This is rust."

I interrupted the routine. "Are your five kids in the audience when you're doing this?" I asked.

She snapped right back, "If they were, I'd be doing better."

After the audience laughed, she continued. "The thing is I did hope to get money, and I still have to take the thrift flight. I hate the thrift flight. It has none of the costly extras—like landing gear. The minute you're in one of these wicker seats—I'm nervous, you know—and by then it's too late—you've got the marks—and, uh—

"The stewardess is eighty-six usually. She said she was one of the Wright Sisters—she built the plane—and I said to her, 'Honey, sweetie'—I'd been shopping at the May Company, and it rubs off—'would you please tell me how long it will be before we get to Los Angeles?' And she said, 'I don't know. We've never made it.'"

PHYLLIS DILLER: You Bet Your Life was a terrifically funny show, and beautifully produced. Look at the care they took in just choosing me. I couldn't tell how often people tell me about seeing the reruns. I never had that much comment on any show I've ever done. Way back then, everybody would say they'd seen it.

On the Dinah Shore show recently, they showed just a teeny little clip from that show. I was horrified at the way I looked. I was nineteen years younger and very skinny, which made my nose look even bigger. My voice was an octave higher, and I was very shy.

But the show still plays. Comedy definitely is timeless. Of course when you run it around again, and it hasn't been seen, it's all new. Comedy is at a premium always. There will never be enough comedy.

A few weeks after Phyllis' appearance, early in 1957, we

had another memorable contestant, Bettina Consolo. She was an old Italian lady trying to find a husband. We brought her back for three weeks running, trying to match her up. She brought increasingly bigger pizzas to be shared with the crew before each appearance.

One of the men we tried to match her up with was Oreste Seragnoli, an Italian Shakespearean actor, and a wonderful, aristocratic old ham. He played along with our matchmaking efforts, having a good time.

He said we should find somebody else for Bettina.

"How do you know you don't want to marry her?" I asked.

Oreste walked around Bettina, which took some time, taking inventory. "Not interested," he firmly said.

You Bet Your Life had been on radio for ten full seasons that spring of 1957. Our combined radio-television audience had reached 35,000,000 people during that period. We'd interviewed 2,100 contestants and given away $700,000 in prize money.

Television was at its peak. Diverse programming was offering viewing fare for the illiterate as well as the intellectual. It was the medium's Golden Age. When we discovered that the great majority of our audience could now afford a television set, it was decided to fold the radio show.

It didn't change my workload any, but it might have lightened that of the technical crew. Occasionally, sight gags that didn't play on radio would have to be eliminated from the radio tape, but kept for television. The staff was in effect putting out two programs every week.

After the advent of the big-money quiz shows, our audience had leveled off. The 1957-1958 season showed a strong recovery, with the audience level matching our peak years of three seasons back, 1954-1955. We accepted this as a sign of getting our proper due. The novelty of huge cash prizes was rapidly wearing off.

I was, somewhat flattered to discover that my imitators weren't doing any better. Edgar Bergen's show folded in January of 1957, while ours remained stronger than ever.

108

It wasn't, however, that we had the ready answers. Edgar discovered that when my Melinda and his Candy appeared in May, 1958, trying to win some money for their pet charity. I sang with the two eleven-and-a-half-year-olds, and then called Edgar out to join us for the quiz.

I agreed to team up with the three others and have George ask the questions.

"We have a surprise for you, Groucho," he said. "We've decided to change the category that you've studied and replace it with a general information quiz composed of questions any sixth grader could answer."

Since I hadn't reached the sixth grade, I was in trouble. So was Edgar, though he'd gone on to college. But the girls did us proud and answered the questions for us.

They won the money for the Girl Scouts. And what did I win? Nothing. In fact, I lost my sponsor.

JOHN GUEDEL: *Actually, there was a problem with DeSoto, because it was at that time a five-thousand-dollar automobile, which today is like an eight-thousand-dollar automobile. It wasn't fair to De-Soto or us, because there was so much wasted audience. Most people couldn't afford to buy a DeSoto. It was a good car, but expensive. It encroached on the Chrysler line on one side, and on the Plymouth and Dodge lines on the other. It was a jazzed-up Dodge or a not-very-far-down Chrysler. We could have taken their other cars and probably done fine. Actually we were sponsored by the dealers, not the factory, though the factory sure as hell controlled it, as far as I could see. Whenever we went to sign anything it was in Detroit, to the head of DeSoto.*

DeSoto was with us on television for eight years. As a matter of fact, we asked them to drop sponsorship. BBD&O had DeSoto and they also had Lever Brothers. Then we sold it to Toni and Lever Brothers, and that time it was really a good buy for them.

It was with neither a whimper nor a bang that we started our twelfth year with the new sponsors. NBC, as part of its promotion, was offering our show and Tennessee Ernie Ford's back-to-back, implying that this hour was a power-house combination.

The big-money quiz shows were on the downgrade.

They'd lost their curiosity value among the American public, at the same time that they became the subject of extreme interest by a New York grand jury.

The furnishing of answers to contestants was revealed, and the whole shabby mess gave all of us in television a black eye. *You Bet Your Life* had fought the inroads of the big-money shows successfully, but we were all tarred by the same brush.

> *MARION POLLOCK: Every show was investigated to see if it was crooked. It would be ridiculous to think that of ours. To begin with, the money was so unimportant. Also, if we wanted to be crooked, the contestants that were matched up would have to know each other, but they met only seconds before they went on the air. Each contestant was interviewed by a different person on the program staff. If one contestant was crooked, he would have to be able to control his partner. This just couldn't happen on our show.*
>
> *An ex-FBI man came to talk to John, Bernie, and Bob—behind closed doors. When the doors were opened, Mrs. Pollock was banned. It was determined that since I wrote the questions and dealt with the contestants before air time, I was the only one who could be crooked. From that point on I was kept in a cocoon in a cage so that I shouldn't corrupt the contestants. It was the first time my integrity had ever been questioned. I cried my eyes out in John's office. He couldn't understand why I was upset.I love Bernie and Bob, and I'm sure they would be shocked to know that it was the most bitter experience of my life.*

I'm also shocked. John, Bernie, and Bob are fully capable of defending themselves, but I feel a word from me is in order.

We all have too high a regard for Marion to do anything that would hurt her. Obviously, we unintentionally did. I say "we" because as the star of the show, the producer and directors were in effect doing my bidding. They are great professionals and I bowed continually to their good judgment.

The investigations showed to us that Marion's spot, since she wrote the questions and also interviewed some of the contestants, was the only conceivable spot where chicanery could occur. To ward off the appearance of evil, and with absolutely no aspersions cast on Marion, it was decided that she would remain as the writer of questions and her spot on the program staff would be reassigned.

That good judgment was confirmed later by the FCC when it laid down rules for quiz shows, one of them being that the person who wrote the questions could have no prior dealings with the contestants. The matter may have been poorly handled, and I hope Marion forgives us.

When so many contrasting temperaments work together as long as we did, it's a wonder we weren't all tearing at one another's hair.We were lucky that we all got along so well. And that some of us still had hair.

In 1959, my autobiography, *Groucho and Me,* was published.

"The success of the show proves what I've always maintained," I wrote. "Talent isn't enough. You have to be lucky. I think if I had my choice of one, I would choose luck. I was lucky to meet this mysterious gentleman . . . John Guedel. . . . And I was lucky to get involved in the kind of show that just seemed to fit my particular talent, small or large as it may be.

"Some of our contestants have gone on to success in show business. Most of them have disappeared into limbo. We have had scientists, musicians, singers, acrobats, an elevator jockey who sang three songs in Sanskrit, a woman who ran a hotel for cats, a man who blew up a large inner tube and then fainted just as the quiz started, an Italian widow whom we deliberately kept on for three successive weeks in hopes that she could snare a husband, and a woman who swam to Catalina and back without stopping. We've had admirals, generals, mayors, statesmen, and tramps. (The tramps were very interesting.) We've had brilliant high school kids, far removed from the beatnik types."

In my narrative I'm singling out guests who are memorable to me. Every night after seeing the show, other great guests come to mind. If I were writing this book a year from now, chances are the guests I'd single out would be entirely different from the ones I'm mentioning now.

It's difficult to keep individual track of them, one show segueing into another, just as one season combined with the next. Soon we were in the Roaring Sixties.

Suddenly I had reached my allotted three-score-and-ten. I still don't know how it happened that I was now living on borrowed time. One day a callow youth and the next on the brink of old age.

During the previous three summers I'd been sowing wild oats—*Time for Elizabeth*. Returning to the stage, acting in a comedy-drama for the first time, was a lesser risk than usual. For I had extreme faith in the playwrights, Norman Krasna and Groucho Marx.

The play had a simple message: to be out of work isn't healthy for a man.

I relished the challenge of one-nighters, acting the part of Ed Davis, the man who retires too soon to Florida and finds himself climbing up the bougainvillaea. He becomes so bored by his inactivity and so exasperated by the other retired people around him that his wife fears he'll commit suicide. "Kill myself?" he replies. "You know we're only covered for fire and theft." At the end of the play he has consented to return to his old job as general manager of a washing machine company.

One of the high spots of those three summers of touring was our playing in Phoenix, Arizona. A distinguished man came backstage to see me. His name was Thornton Wilder. What did one of America's greatest playwrights think of the newest member of his fraternity? I waited, awe-struck, for his answer. "You should have ad libbed more," he advised.

While in Phoenix, I became aware that one of its leading citizens was a shameless joke-snatcher. A story much repeated about my misadventures revolves around the refusal of an exclusive southern California beach club to accept me as a member because I'm Jewish.

"Since my daughter is only half Jewish," I asked, "could she go into the water up to her knees?"

Barry Goldwater, now Arizona's senior United States Senator, was similarly refused membership in a golf club. "Since I'm only half-Jewish," he wrote, "can I play nine holes?" I guess that's what they mean when they describe Goldwater as a physical conservative.

If that weren't bad enough (I don't mean my outrageous pun, but Goldwater's plagiarism), I was getting quite a bit of insubordination at home.

> *MELINDA MARX BERTI: Even when I first started going on the show I was aware of tremendous pressure. During later times it became very intense and uncomfortable and something I didn't want to do at all.*
>
> *I think I appeared about once a year until I was twelve or thirteen. But I was simply not stagestruck. I felt I was being held up for judgment and ridicule. The kids at school could be pretty cruel.*
>
> *You have to realize I had stage parents on both sides. My mother's family had come to Hollywood because she was an aspiring actress. As a result I was taught singing and dancing and acrobatics. It was a very automatic thing, and I was twelve years old before I realized what was going on.*
>
> *When I would tell Groucho later that I was uncomfortable and didn't want to do it, he would say, "You don't have to." And of course get his way.*

I don't know how many times I stamped my feet or threatened to hold my breath, but these tactics weren't fooling Melinda any more.

I'd already written my autobiography, and had gone out on summer tours. I needed the challenge of something new, and I found it in something deliciously old.

I've always been a Gilbert & Sullivan fan, and there are traces of their influence in the songs I've sung in movies.

I'd now be singing on television—seriously that is—playing Ko-Ko, the Lord High Executioner, in *The Mikado*. My costars would be operatic diva Helen Traubel, playing Katisha, and Dennis King as the Mikado. I loved the experience, and if it made new fans for Gilbert & Sullivan, that was ample reward. The show was produced by my best friend, Goddard Lieberson.

On April 29, 1960, we invited a special guest, Lena Marciano, to be on the show. She was the mother of heavyweight champion Rocky Marciano. She was paired with the Reverend James Whitcomb Brougher, an upright Baptist minister. Lena was charming, but Reverend Brougher . . .
My exchange with him went like this:

GROUCHO

How old are you?

REVEREND

I'll be ninety years old on January seventh.

GROUCHO

That's wonderful. I want to shake hands with a man who's even older than I am. How about the ladies, Doc? Are you a gay bachelor or are you in the trap?

REVEREND

I'm in the trap.

GROUCHO

Well, how old is Mrs. Brougher?

REVEREND

Well, Mrs. Brougher is sixty-nine. She's twenty-one years younger than me.

GROUCHO

You're a cradle snatcher, aren't you? Married a kid twenty years younger than you.

REVEREND

Yes, I'd rather smell perfume than liniment.

GROUCHO

I would too unless I had arthritis. You seem to be a pretty active fellow, Doc. Does your wife keep up with this fast pace?

Here I am during my first season of *You Bet Your Life* on ABC radio. (David Zalkus collection)

My partners in crime during the third season on CBS radio: First row, Edward T. Tyler, Gummo Marx, Bernie Smith, unidentified, John Guedel, Dorothy Nye, yours truly, Robert Dwan, Hy Freedman, Carroll Nye, the CBS sound effects man, the CBS unit manager; second row, Edwin I. Mills, sound engineer John Neal, unidentified, Jerry Fielding, George Fenneman. (Bernie Smith collection)

I was named Outstanding Television Personality of 1949 by the Academy of Television Arts and Sciences. The awards were so new that when I was told Emmy was mine, I reached for the girl instead of the statuette.

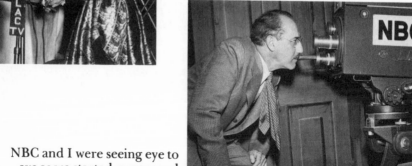

NBC and I were seeing eye to eye as we started our second television season in 1951.

The fancy hood ornament on my 1952 DeSoto was my daughter Melinda. I accepted delivery of the car (I received two of them a year) from my friendly Dodge-DeSoto dealer. The grille, you will notice, looks like a set of bad teeth.

Groucho's Top Value Used Cars. Are you sure Madman Muntz started this way? (Photo by Cover Studio)

Tell them Groucho sent you. (I hope he still does.)

The Thinker starts his third season on NBC. (David Zalkus collection)

Pedro Gonzalez Gonzalez was one of the earliest "civilian stars" on our show. He later joined "the service" and was under personal contract to John Wayne for many years. Some say he was the funniest guest ever to appear on *You Bet Your Life*. (Pedro Gonzalez Gonzalez collection)

The secret word is Ouch!

Fenneman as Peter Pan. Mary Martin didn't lose any sleep.

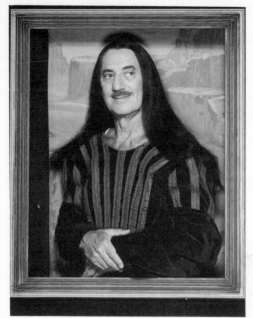

Mona and I had the same wistful smile. (Bernie Smith collection)

Am I blue? (Bernie Smith Collection)

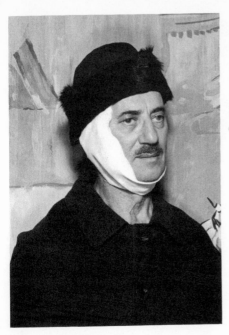

Ear ache.
(Bernie Smith collection)

Actually, I look more
like my mother.
(Bernie Smith collection)

Monte Montana and his horse. Loved his horse.

Well, I'll be a monkey's uncle! (Bernie Smith collection)

"You're an interesting young couple, and it's been fun talking to you . . . Now which category . . . ."
(Courtesy Virgil Partch)

Melinda danced with her proud father on many shows.

I learn to shimmy like my sister Kate. That's my sister Kate.

Crazylegs Rowena was our most eccentric dancer. After her appearance, Irwin Allen signed her to a studio contract.

GROUCHO: You plan to stand on your head?
CONTESTANT: Yes, but I'll need a little room.
GROUCHO: Well, stand on your head. We'll get you a little room later.

Our long-suffering program staff: Dorothy Nye, Bernie Smith, E. T. "Doc" Tyler, Hy Freedman, and Eddie Mills. (Bernie Smith collection)

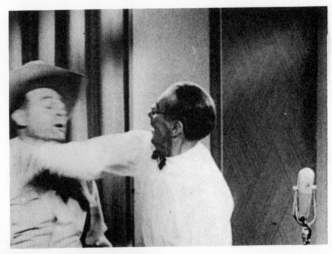

Crash Corrigan didn't smile when he said that.

Harry Ruby is the man I loved. We sang together on the show. When he died, part of me died too.

Composer Sammy Cahn.

The Family Hour. Edgar Bergen and I answer questions any sixth grader could answer. Quizmaster is George Fenneman. Edgar and I each brought our own sixth graders, daughters Candice and Melinda, both age eleven and a half.

Harpo's only appearance on the show, to promote his autobiography. He always made me laugh.

Christmas, 1961. The day after Christmas, I used the carcass for *Duck Soup.* (NBC photo by Herb Ball)

GEORGE FENNEMAN: Groucho, you were kind of proud of me, weren't you—like when I'd win an award or something?
GROUCHO: I wasn't proud of you. I was disgraced. (NBC photo by Paul Bailey)

Olympic decathlon
champion Robert Mathias.
(Bernie Smith collection)

My favorite musician, the man who played the
tube.

Housewife-comedienne Phyllis Diller, who made her first national television appearance on *You Bet Your Life.*

Singer Gladys Bentley. She really could shake her hips.

The immortal Esther Bradley.

And thanks to you and all our contestants.

A reunion at my eighty-fifth birthday party with Bernie Smith, George Fenneman, Howard Harris, and Robert Dwan.

REVEREND

She goes wherever I go—men's clubs—

GROUCHO

She goes with you to men's clubs?

REVEREND

Yes, I'm so homely. She'd rather go along than kiss me good-bye.

GROUCHO

Doc, I want to ask you a question. Have you ever had a blood transfusion from Milton Berle? What kind of minister are you?

REVEREND

I've been preaching the gospel of Christ for seventy years, and I'm a Baptist preacher, and past president of the American Baptist Convention, which is the largest honor a man in my field can receive.

GROUCHO

What made you decide to become a minister when you could have been an old renegade like me? I'm no good, you know, no good at all. . . .

REVEREND

Yes, well, my father and mother wanted me to be a preacher. Friends wanted me to be a comedian, and, Groucho, if I had, I would have preceded you.

GROUCHO

Nobody's preceded me. Look, if you like I'll switch spots with you.

REVEREND

And nobody can succeed you. (Ha, ha, ha)

GROUCHO

The salary they pay you ministers, you'd better have a sense of humor or a rich wife.

REVEREND

I went to cash a check the other day and the banker counted out some old money. He said, "Are you afraid of germs?" I said, "No. No germ could live on the salary I get."

GROUCHO

You know, I didn't know that they cracked jokes like that in the Baptist church. I thought it was all hellfire and brimstone.

REVEREND

It depends. If they need that, we give it to them.

(Reverend Brougher and I got serious for a while, and he proceeded to explain his calling. As we continued):

GROUCHO

Do you utilize your sense of humor in your preaching?

REVEREND

Yes, I do.

GROUCHO

In what way? Do you say, "A funny thing happened to me on the way to the church?"

REVEREND

No, I went up to San Francisco to a benefit, and I was getting dressed in my room when a knock came at the door and a man came in all dressed up in his tuxedo. He said, "I'm going to introduce you, Doctor, and I want to know something about you. Also, I'll take you to the banquet room." I said, "Fine, but I'm just tying my bow tie. Can you tie one of these bow ties so that it stands straight?" He said, "You bet I can." He came over and put his arms around me, lay me on the bed and tied it, and I got up. I said, "That's fine and dandy, but why did you make me lie down on the bed?" He said, "That's the only way I can do it. I'm an undertaker."

GROUCHO

Well, that's certainly a holier than thou attitude. Do you have any more jokes up your sleeve, Rev? You don't care if I call you Rev?

REVEREND

Yes. People enjoy jokes told on yourself. They're getting so sensitive I can't tell a joke on the Jews or the colored people or an Irishman.

GROUCHO

This is true. It goes even further than that. If you tell a joke about a dentist, or a plumber, or anybody at all.

132

REVEREND

So you tell jokes about yourself.

GROUCHO

I can't tell a joke about an Irishman on myself.

REVEREND

Anyway, one night about midnight I was going home, and I saw a friend of mine on the sidewalk, and he'd made the mistake of taking something in his stomach that made him see double and think half. I said, "I'd better take you home." So I got him out in front of his house, got him up the steps, and rang the bell. And I said, "Now, Bill, I'd better go." He grabbed me and said, "No, no. Don't you go yet. You wait until my wife comes to the door. I want her to see who I've been out with tonight."

GROUCHO

The Baptist church is going to get a lot of converts tonight. There's going to be a lot of water spilled around here. We ought to go into business together. You give the jokes and sermons and I'll take the collection, and we'll split fifty-fifty. I take the cash and I'll leave you the buttons.

REVEREND

Let me tell you one more. An old man had heart trouble, and he bought an Irish Sweepstakes ticket. And he won fifty thousand dollars, but his wife and daughter were afraid he would drop dead when he heard the news. So they called a clergyman to come and tell him. So he came and they talked a few minutes. Finally, he said, "John, didn't you buy a ticket for the sweepstakes?" He said, "Yes, I did." The clergyman said, "Now suppose you should win fifty thousand dollars. What would you do with it?" The old man said, "If I won fifty thousand dollars, I'd give half of it to you." And the preacher dropped dead!

EDWIN I. MILLS: *I thought it would be great to have Margaret Dumont on the show. She was in retirement, and I went to see her. It got to the painful point where we had to talk about money. Our attitude was that if the contestants got paid to come on it wouldn't be as spon-*

taneous a thing. They were freer. I didn't know how to approach it with her, and neither did she. She was the grande dame, lovely little thing. And so we never had her on the show. It's one of my greatest regrets.

The season ended with a couple winning the $10,000 grand prize. That wasn't so unusual, but one of the pair was Mrs. Oney Boren, who put her $5,000 in sugar futures. She subsequently made $200,000.

When we prepared for the tenth television season, NBC felt we'd better have a big push. Ratings had been slipping for the last couple of seasons and it was decided we needed a boost.

NBC published a prospectus of the show, just as if we were a new stock offering.

Several new gimmicks would be introduced on *The New Groucho Show*. While stressing that our show was only one of four keeping its hold on the viewing public for over ten years (the others were Jack Benny, Ed Sullivan, and *What's My Line?*), the network didn't hesitate in revamping a proven winner.

Working in tandem with our producer and directors, NBC came up with the idea of a Mrs. Development House contest in cooperation with Junior Chambers of Commerce and NBC station promotion departments in twenty-five major cities. A "black box" mystery feature would also be introduced. I would be making a different, zany grand entrance each week.

The Untouchables on ABC was perilously close to topping our ratings the previous season. We'd maintained a 39 percent share of the audience to their 38 percent share, with the CBS *Playhouse 90* a weak third at 23 percent.

When all the glitter had settled, we were back in business at the same old stand with the same old format.

BERNIE SMITH: There was a joke in the Reader's Digest. *A man named Sexauer was working in a department store. Somebody called, and asked, "Do you have a Sexauer there?" The girl who an-*

swered the phone said, "Sex hour? We have a hard enough time getting a coffee break." That joke always killed me. Then the kids came to me one time with a contestant named Sexauer from Alaska. That's our man, I thought. We got him on for just the one joke. He was kind of amusing, but the joke never got on the air.

Apparently, the only intimation of sex we'd allow was the one suggestion adopted from the prospectus, now renamed the Mrs. Housing Development contest. We had housewives parading in swimsuits during much of our eleventh television season.

The first week of December didn't pass unnoticed by our staff. At that time, DeSoto stopped production. The 1961 model then in DeSoto-Plymouth showrooms would be the last ever.

Someone mentioned that we'd already put Elgin-American Compacts out of business. And now we'd run DeSoto into the ground. Fortunately, Toni Home Permanents and Old Gold cigarettes, our current sponsors, weren't superstitious, and continued bearing with us.

We pressed on as 1961 rolled around. In Washington, Kennedy's New Frontier policies were being developed just as we in California on *You Bet Your Life* were defending our old ones.

Our ratings that January had dropped to their lowest. Homes reached were 9,660,000, and our number of TV homes in program station areas were now 20.6 percent. The writing was on the wall.

Somehow we managed to get through the year.

At least a couple more memorable contestants would be on the show.

On February 9, a handsome, swarthy man came on and was introduced as a visiting Arabian prince. He was wearing sunglasses, which he declined to take off.

The prince proceeded to talk about his father's four wives and of his countless half-brothers and sisters. He had us all fooled for a while, but then we caught on to his game.

I eyed him suspiciously. "I think you've made this whole thing up," I said. "You're no more Arabian than I am. What do you think about that?"

"I'm a prince at heart, Groucho," he replied. "And actually my mother was an Arab."

"It was pretty obvious to me you aren't an Arabian," I went on, "because I used to have an Arabian horse and I know what they look like. Well, who are you?"

"Actually, I'm Bill Blatty—"

"Are you a wolf in sheep's clothing?" I interjected.

"In sheikh's clothing," he corrected. He went on to explain that he was an old friend of Fenneman's and had played this charade at several Hollywood parties. "George told me you're the world's greatest authority on spotting phonies," Blatty said, "and he sort of egged me on to put you to the test tonight."

"I have no knack for spotting phonies," I said. "Fenneman was wrong. He's been in my employ for fourteen years and I haven't spotted him yet."

Blatty was a clever fellow, and he and his partner won the grand prize of $10,000 at the end of the show.

"What are you going to do with the money?" I asked him.

"It's going to finance me to finish my book," he replied.

The rest, as they say, is history. With his money he was able to buy a middle name, and as William Peter Blatty became famous some years later as the author of *The Exorcist.*

A few weeks later Harpo made his only appearance on the show. He came on to plug his autobiography, *Harpo Speaks,* performed some tomfoolery with Fenneman, and retired to the wings. That should have been my cue.

The season limped along to a conclusion. Our last show, Number 528, aired on June 29, 1961. The last contestants were a couple named Molly Magruder and Jerry Shannon.

During the height of our run, there was never any thought that we wouldn't be renewed each season. The job had become a sinecure for all of us. But now, the ratings told the story.

136

The show was not renewed. It wasn't *The Untouchables* that did us in, nor a hay-burner whose name I forget, since the TV westerns seemed to be composed of interchangeable, indistinguishable stars.

Our format had become too familiar, and the public was ready for something new. After fourteen years, so was I.

I took the fall of 1961 to make up my mind.

Tell It to Groucho. It came to Guedel in a flash. This would be a new type of audience participation show, in which contestants would appear to talk about some problem facing them. I, with the help of the studio audience, would offer some advice. A quiz segment was attached to the format, but again it wasn't the most important part of the show.

CBS had told us they would buy a show starring myself if we had a new format. We began broadcasting on January 11, 1962.

Contestants were provided a platform to talk about their favorite causes. The network thought we needed the crutch of more celebrities than we'd had on *You Bet Your Life,* and several prominent people came on the program: Ken Berry, Mayor Sam Yorty of Los Angeles, Mary Astor, Peter Lorre, Jayne Mansfield and Mickey Hargitay, Rod Serling, Wendell Corey, and Vincent Price.

We broadcast twenty shows altogether, before the series ended on May 24. It nearly finished me too.

When such a sizable portion of one's life has been devoted to an enterprise like *You Bet Your Life,* there are thousands of memories that keep bumping into each other. In general, mine were extremely happy and positive. The people I worked with were that often-used but seldom merited adjective, true professionals, and that's how I remember them. As to how they remember me, well—

ROBERT DWAN: Do you know my favorite tribute from Groucho? Once, he says to me, "Dwan, I have nothing but admiration for you and very little of that." I treasure that. Another time I asked him for his favorite line. He said, "Stone walls do not a Jackson make."

137

BERNIE SMITH: *People have always asked me what it was like to work for Groucho. Usually they would ask, "Wasn't he a monster to work for?" I don't know why they feel that. They might think because he was so overpowering he would be very sharp and caustic, which he wasn't. Generally I'd tell them, "Groucho is as regular as an old shoe. He's just like any other internationally known multimillionaire star. In fact, he puts his trousers on just like the rest of us, one cloven hoof at a time."*

JACK MEAKIN: *One year I went to this fancy gourmet place here in Beverly Hills and I sent Groucho a big smoked turkey for a Christmas present. So he wrote me back a note, which read: "The smoked turkey you sent me is great. I've never smoked one before, but I'm going to try as soon as the holidays are over."*

JOHN GUEDEL: *I guess Groucho must have called me on camera a dozen times or more. I loved it, because I'm a ham. He would always introduce me very seriously: "This is the producer." It always involved how we would handle the money. Invariably I'd say, "We'll give the money to both of them." Groucho would say, "Big shot. He's not giving his money. If it was his, he wouldn't give it to either one of them."*

EDWIN I. MILLS: *Groucho showed literally no temperament. He was the pro at all times. Consequently, the organization was always close. We weren't traveling agents. Those who started on the show ended it. It was a career for all of us.*

He never had to psych himself up for the show. Groucho didn't try to be too funny. The minute he'd walk off the show, he'd be his own very quiet man.

One day, after all those years, Groucho looked at me and said, "Ed, you've grown bald in the service." And I had.

JERRY FIELDING: *Groucho gave Christmas presents to everyone, and mine one year was membership in a thing called "The Cheese of the Month Club." I got a smelly cheese every month. I think that was the first year we were on the show. He didn't keep that up after a while. By and large I got the feeling that, although he felt the show was easy and worth a lot of money to him, it wasn't really what he would have preferred to do. That's why I think he went out and did that play every year.*

138

I think Groucho in his own way has a much higher intellectual level than most people who do quiz shows. And I'm sure he had a vile inner contempt for what he was doing and for half of the idiots that appeared. That's why he appeared to be mean to some of them. He could get away with it because they never believed he meant it.

BERNIE SMITH: *I remember one of the very rare times that Groucho broke up on the show. We had a housewife on as a contestant. She was a very aggressive, dominant personality, and she had a number of things in mind to say to him. This, of course, we always encouraged.*

She was talking away, and Groucho—predictably—started to interrupt her. She turned to him and said, "Groucho, you're stepping on my lines." And this coming from a housewife. It really floored him for a minute. He turned to Dwan and me, raised his eyebrows, and said, "The contestants are striking back."

ROBERT DWAN: *He would never tell a toilet joke, you know. He had a lot of good taste, he really did. My editing was largely, as I say, the device to let him go free and have conversations. If they weren't funny, then we just didn't broadcast them, that's all.*

JERRY FIELDING: *Groucho frequently made jokes at other people's expense, but he never put me on much. He never played with my dignity, which he seemed to sense was rather important to me. So I never really had too much of a close collaboration with him. I got a feeling there was a general tacit understanding between us, that he knew what I was about and I knew what he was about, and not much ever needed to be said. They were nice years. It was a nicer world then than it is now.*

ROBERT DWAN: *We usually went to Chasen's for dinner after the show. One night we were there and right behind a booth, in a dining alcove, some people were having a birthday party. Waiters wheeled in a cake. Groucho got up and stopped him and proceeded to serve the cake himself. No one at the next table noticed who he was. He just served it, came back to our table, and sat down. It only proves no one pays attention to waiters.*

BERNIE SMITH: *Before he grew a mustache and people started recognizing him, few people asked Groucho for his autograph.*

Consequently, he was always gracious about signing them.
We were at the Derby waiting for a table. A little old lady came up.
She'd just had her hair done in tight little ringlets. She shoved an auto-
graph book under Groucho's nose. She asked, "Are you Harpo Marx?"
Groucho looked at her, completely cold. "No, I'm not," he said. "Are
you?"

Later in 1962, NBC took another look at our show and decided to syndicate. Because of some legal problems we selected only the shows from 1955 on, and started the rerun circuit with *The Best of Groucho.*

JOHN GUEDEL: Those years were 1962 to 1965, roughly. Then they stopped syndicating it because they said nobody wanted to buy it. Groucho would call me and say, "Can't you get them to do some more? We have a better show than those that are now on." Periodically I'd try to get them to do something, and periodically they'd tell me they couldn't sell it. "In the first place, color is in now. In the second place, they're old-fashioned. And that's that."
They weren't really trying very hard. For there was a lot of money that had to be spent on residuals. If they made one sale, they were sup-posed to have to spend seventy thousand dollars, they said, for music rights and musicians. I took their word for it. Actually they hadn't looked into it too deeply because that hasn't been the case.

Though I hadn't performed in several years, outside of a few talk show appearances, my name and face were still be-fore the public through the syndication. Now that had end-ed. I signed to host *The Hollywood Palace* at around income tax time in 1965. Margaret Dumont came on as a special guest. We re-created the "Captain Spaulding" number from *Animal Crackers.* A few weeks later she was dead. She was a wonderful woman and a fine actress. I loved her.

The quiz had never played abroad, although yours truly did. Many a broad.

We did a spinoff of *You Bet Your Life* when we went to England in the fall of 1965. Guedel, Dwan, and Smith were also involved in the venture. The formula didn't work, and we folded our tents after thirteen weeks.

> *BERNIE SMITH: In England you don't call up strangers and ask them if they want to be on Groucho's show. So you invite friends and friends of friends. We would have run out of contestants if the show hadn't been dropped after thirteen weeks.*
>
> *It was a funny thing. Groucho is a big star in England, and yet the show didn't go. British humor is very broad, and they couldn't reconcile the Hackenbush and Spaulding characters with this middle-aged, cerebral man.*
>
> *After one of the shows Groucho turned to me and said, "It's a whole audience of mothers-in-law out there. They don't have the faintest idea of what I'm talking about."*

My career in England has been somewhat checkered. When the Marx Brothers first went to England, we put on a new act there, called *On the Balcony*. We worked for forty-eight minutes and got three laughs.

The audience began to throw pennies onto the stage. I stepped to the footlights. "We've come a long way," I told them. "The least you could do is throw silver."

Then we went back to an old act, called *Home Again*, which they loved.

The next few years were to be spent in semiretirement. I'd returned to the United States to discover that the Library of Congress had asked me to donate my personal papers, manuscripts, and correspondence. I began compiling them. Out of these efforts came a book, called *The Groucho Letters*, which was published in 1967.

> *ROBERT DWAN: A few years ago I passed by the old studio at Sunset and Vine. It's where that Home Savings place is now. Honest to gosh, it was just at that moment when the wrecking ball, on the end of one of those great big derrick things, was going through Studio A, at the point where Groucho used to sit on his stool. I saw them knocking it down and it was spooky.*

I guess I could have stayed retired, saving up enough trading stamps to buy a toaster and swapping lies with my cronies at Hillcrest Country Club. But I had the great good sense not to want to stagnate.

My Carnegie Hall concert in 1972 was a sensation with the kids. Half the audience was dressed as the Marx Brothers.

I personally didn't doubt the extent of my popularity. When *Animal Crackers* was rereleased early in 1974, I went to New York for the opening. The mob scene was unbelievable, and thrilling. Policemen on horses had to be brought in to keep the crowd under control. One of the horses asked for my autograph. I gave him a horse laugh.

So now, they tell me, I'm a cult. Revivals of the Marx Brothers films are playing to sold-out houses all over the world. The boom in Groucho-related merchandise exceeds the Davy Crockett craze of twenty years ago. The reruns of *You Bet Your Life* are top-rated in their time slots in virtually every market in which they appear.

A few months ago *TV Guide* ran an article about the revival of television shows of the fifties. It stated that *You Bet Your Life* and *Mickey Mouse Club* are the great hits.

The article went on to say that our show was revived when John Guedel called John T. Reynolds, who runs KTLA in Los Angeles, and asked him to rerun the shows so that I wouldn't have to drag out my projector to watch them. Instead I could just turn on the TV set.

Said and done, according to *TV Guide*. If I'd known that the only motive of profit-hungry television stations was to mollify a man approaching middle age, then I would have also requested the return of *Omnibus*.

I'm not ungrateful, however, that the show is running again, for it gives me a chance to remember people. Watching the show is a happy alternative to the eleven o'clock news, with its recap of the catastrophic events of the day. It's hardly the stuff that makes for sweet dreams. Consequently, I'm one of the millions who also watches the show every night.

JOHN GUEDEL: NBC was going to destroy the film in August of

1973. They called and asked me, "Would you like to have a set of films for your garage as mementos of the show?" I said, "What do you mean?" They said, "We're destroying them to make room in our ware-house in New Jersey." I said, "You're kidding. How many have you destroyed so far?" They said fifteen of two hundred fifty negatives. I said, "Stop! Right now! Let me talk to New York." I called them and said, "Look. You don't want to syndicate. I'll ask Groucho to be part-ners. I'll give you royalties for every station we sign up." We made a deal. So we have it for three years, and we can renew it for three years. By six years I'm sure we will have run it out again.

John and I had previously tried to interest NBC in syn-dicating the show. But we were informed that the show was too slow and old-fashioned, and also in black and white, which today's audiences don't like.

I knew that our show was as funny as anything on the air. Whenever guests would come to dinner, they'd insist on see-ing some of the programs in my projection room. They couldn't fake their obvious enjoyment, and if this was their reaction, then the American public would also find them amusing.

As a result of some government edict, NBC was forced to get out of the syndication business, and sold its library to NTA. This second organization had no interest in syndicat-ing the show, and NBC needed the warehouse space, so the next step was to throw them in the bonfire.

John and I made a royalty deal to syndicate the show, and NBC agreed to ship all their prints and negatives to us. They were shipped to Erin Fleming and stored in her garage. My grandson Andy Marx had just graduated from UCLA and was looking for a job, so John and I hired him to screen the programs and put them in some semblance of order.

In the meantime, Guedel tried to sell it to several stations. He got turndowns from all of them.

Finally, John Reynolds, president of KTLA, Channel 5 in Los Angeles, agreed to take a thirteen-week chance and put *The Best of Groucho* on at eleven o'clock.

It was hardly a calculated risk for Channel 5. The station was paying only $54.88 a broadcast for the show. When the first ratings came in, we knew we had something, and we could now renegotiate.

Meanwhile, basing their reverse decisions on the success of the Channel 5 experiment, other television stations started signing up. We struck new prints from the negatives and started doing business.

JOHN GUEDEL: My first thought in wanting to resell the show was the nostalgia craze. I felt we would get all the same audience again. Groucho is basically funny, and he is a rare individual. I thought there might be a plus because Erin Fleming has arranged Groucho very well to do all kinds of publicity and tours for young people, at the colleges and at Carnegie Hall. All this emphasis on young people, and they were cottoning to him because he's a balloon pricker. So he became their darling. So I thought maybe he'd get that audience too. But being on at eleven at night, I think that's probably our main audience, because the original audience I'm talking about gets pretty sleepy at eleven o'clock at night.

The show is now on nine of the top ten markets, and is airing on about forty-five. The reason it's not on so many is because it's become an eleven o'clock show, and it's very difficult to get on a network station because the networks are locked in with the news. No network station is willing to give up the news to the other two networks. Sooner or later one of them is going to say, "Come on, fellows. Let's be smart and counterprogram at this hour rather than fight head-on."

As a result, we have a hard time getting in three-station cities where there are all network stations. We're finally breaking in on late afternoon time on some of the network stations, but mainly we have to go to towns where there are four or more stations. Obviously, those are very big cities only. However, we hit more than sixty percent of the population right now. I think the show will be in all English-speaking countries eventually. There's great interest in it.

MARION POLLOCK: Whenever they have a podium that's sort of circular, I think, "Oh, boy, my name is going to be on there." I've published three textbooks and written over thirty articles. My students are far more impressed by the fact my name is on the show than anything I've achieved since then. We're a glamor-struck society. We elect movie stars for governors and Senators, but I hope not for President.

144

What the public is seeing is a slightly abridged version of *You Bet Your Life*. Since the shows were shot for prime time, they left a three-minute hole for commercials per half hour.

On late night television, however, the hole can be six minutes. Three minutes from the original shows are missing from those now being seen, and I hope they don't seem as choppy to the public as they do to me. They obviously don't, since we've had no complaints yet.

> *ROBERT DWAN: Nobody else would be worried about this, but, you know, we had a sign on the back wall. It said "DeSoto-Plymouth Dealers." Later on as we got classy we put it on the front of the podium, and that lasted for a long, long time. Finally we got bright and for the last couple of years we photographed the show without the sign on the back wall, and then optically inserted it on the master shot, wherever it was supposed to appear. I had it photographed so that we didn't show that area any other time.*
>
> *When the show went into syndication with other sponsors, the signs had to be eliminated. NBC took the first big bunch of shows and optically blew the pictures up. So, like on the Esther Bradley show, which I saw last night, it has her way over on the side of the screen. An awful lot of shots show her talking to somebody, but you don't see anybody else.*
>
> *We used lots of headroom. I was very careful to put plenty of air space around because I knew that especially in the early days nobody had his set adjusted right. You'd never have any problem on the close-ups or on the tight two-shots. But a lot of time it would be an inside two-shot, the shot with Groucho and the person standing next to him, and you could see a piece of that sign on the back wall. Well, the dummies blew the thing up so that Esther Bradley is over here about half on. I'm dying, because I didn't photograph it that way. I wish I could run a disclaimer at the end of the thing: "It wasn't my fault."*

I guess no account of *You Bet Your Life* would be complete without listing the current professional associations of my colleagues on the show. Curiously, none of them are involved in the regular grind of a television series. I took care of that.

* * *

WHATEVER HAPPENED TO DEPARTMENT:

John Guedel is chairman of the board of Test, Inc., Northridge, California, manufacturer of electronic equipment.

Robert Dwan is executive vice-president of Atkins-Gilbert, Beverly Hills production company.

Bernie Smith is a partner in Dennis James Productions, Hollywood, and producer of television commercials for that company.

George Fenneman won a 1974 Emmy as host of *Talk About Pictures*. He is currently hosting *On Campus* for NBC, and is a spokesman for Home Savings and Loan, as well as for other commercial enterprises.

Hy Freedman is general manager of Los Angeles television station KVST-TV, Channel 68.

E. T. "Doc" Tyler, after leaving the show, became an international authority on fertility and was one of the developers of the birth control pill. He died in August, 1975.

Jerry Fielding established a distinguished career as a composer and film scorer, and was nominated for Academy Awards for his scores of *Straw Dogs* and *The Wild Bunch*.

Edwin I. Mills is affiliated with Pitney-Bowes, Santa Maria, California.

Marion Pollock is a full professor at California State University at Long Beach, and graduate coordinator of the Health Education Program.

Jack Meakin is director of advertising and public relations of Film Communicators, North Hollywood producer and distributor of nontheatrical films.

Howard Harris, after several years of association with the Suicide Prevention Center of Los Angeles, has retired.

If my career isn't as active as it once was, you couldn't prove it by the American public. Every time I turn around I see myself in previous incarnations, all Seven Ages of Man there for me to see at the same time.

MELINDA MARX BERTI: Groucho was a funny man. He

made people laugh. He broke conformity and the established rules. Anybody who can make somebody laugh makes the world better.

EDGAR BERGEN: Groucho, through the years, is probably the fastest comedian on ad libs. He just throws them at you, good and bad. As he said, "If you tell a bad joke or pun, you just gotta expect that once in a while."

I think Groucho will be remembered for his sparkling, fast delivery. He's told an awful lot of jokes worth repeating. I still hear "an elephant in my pajamas." That has been borrowed and replayed. The brothers had the advantage that I did, of vaudeville, to time it and to keep it moving.

Question: What is timing?

It means giving the pause or that beat where it'll mean the most, and where it will help the joke. For example, if you want to throw them away and do them fast, that's fine. Jack Benny, though, had that stare and that look. I like to play with a line. Charlie and Mortimer don't give me the answer right straight back. Mortimer, for example, will say, "Well, I, uh—yeah—uh—well." I say, "Thinking doesn't come very easy to you, does it?" He answers, "Uhh—no, no it doesn't. I always get the feeling that I'm thinking against the wind, you see."

Question: What about some of Groucho's lines, which on the face of it aren't funny?

I think that's just a personal style of delivery. He gives you subtle comedy, obvious comedy, but he gives it to you fast. I would say All in the Family and Maude today would be the style of the thing that he would do in those days.

PHYLLIS DILLER: You realize my cigarette holder is Groucho's cigar, and my hair is Harpo's fright wig. So the Marx Brothers, and Groucho particularly, since he was the comedian of the group, have influenced me. All new comics can learn from their peers, and the people who came before, because you don't go to college to study comedy.

Groucho's delivery, and the way he lays a line out: That's where you study comedy. He could take a line and people would laugh. If somebody else said it, there wouldn't be a laugh. Now we're working with attitude, plus that cigar and those eyes. It's looking at this embodied attitude. He's a legend in his own time.

MORRIE RYSKIND: We reminisce and, of course, when you get

to be our age, that's great fun. I think what we all remember are the tough times. Groucho delights in telling about the time the manager didn't pay them. At the time it wasn't very funny, but those are the things you remember, because you conquered them, I guess. Nobody says, "Well, I opened in your show, it was a great show and it got great reviews, and we all went home and lived happily ever after." We say, "Do you remember when that son of a bitch tried to do that to us?"

What did Groucho stand for basically? He was the guy who said the king has no clothes on, the guy who couldn't stand the stuffed shirt. And he could say it like nobody else could.

I write a newspaper column. I often wish that I could have Groucho say some of those words. I know that the laughs he would get would be much bigger. He was superb at that.

I don't think there was a basic difference in the characters he played in movies and the Groucho we saw on television. He used the same attack. He'd get the poor guy up there and by the time he got through ribbing him, well. . . . He went after Fenneman pretty well, and that was the fun of it. When he made Fenneman seem like a little pup, the audience loved it. For at the end, Groucho always had some graciousness to make up for it.

I occasionally find myself lapsing in real life, back to the role of quizmaster, as I did on a recent day when George Fenneman came to lunch. The Inquisition went like this:

GROUCHO
Where were you born?

GEORGE
I was born in Peking, China.

GROUCHO
China, huh?

GEORGE
Yeah, and that was a thing that never in our fifteen years together did you let me forget.

GROUCHO
Where's my laundry?

GEORGE
(To onlookers) See, that's one of them. And every time he'd meet my wife, he'd say, "Is it true what they say about you Chinese women?" Groucho would accuse me of having a De-

Soto with a trunk full of egg foo yung. He said he would always tell it was my car, because there'd be laundry in the back seat. (*To Groucho*) Groucho, you were kind of proud of me too, weren't you? Like when I'd win an award or something?

GROUCHO

I wasn't proud of you. I was disgraced.

GEORGE

(*To onlookers*) Well, that's what I mean. Now I've learned to read those lines for what they are—love. Otherwise, I'd cry a lot.

GROUCHO

How did you get in the profession, or racket, that you're in?

GEORGE

It *is* a racket. I was going to be a teacher.

GROUCHO

What kind of teacher?

GEORGE

I was going to be a speech and drama teacher. And then I got married and my wife was a teacher and she brought home ninety-two dollars a month, and I realized that I didn't want to work for ninety-two dollars a month, so I—

GROUCHO

Took a pay cut?

GEORGE

So I took a pay cut and I worked for thirty-five dollars a week at KSFO in San Francisco. That was my first announcing job.

GROUCHO

How'd you get to be an announcer?

GEORGE

I auditioned a lot and I had a San Francisco accent which is kind of a New York–Boston accent. They say Mah-ket Street, because there was a big Irish contingent in San Francisco. I went to school with a lot of Irish kids. Anyway, I had to get rid of it. I finally got into the business after auditioning a lot, and I remember my first job. It was—

GROUCHO

About China—were you there a long time?

GEORGE

Well, you know, I was there for nine months. I don't remember anything about it and my parents came back to San Francisco.

GROUCHO

Why were you born there?

GEORGE

Here's a Groucho line! I wanted to be near my mother. My father was in import-export. They'd been married for ten years. I guess they didn't expect any children and I'm an only child, which accounts for some of my decency and goodness.

GROUCHO

So then—

GEORGE

Then I grew up in San Francisco.

GROUCHO

You drove from China to San Francisco? Quite a drive.

GEORGE

Got on a big boat, I understand.

GROUCHO

How do you drive from China?

GEORGE

No, you get on a boat or a rickshaw.

GROUCHO

It's a long way.

I should know. It's been a long way in my own life.

My regrets are few. I'm sorry Harpo and Chico and Sam and Minnie are dead. They taught me how to laugh.

What a thrill it must have been for Minnie to see her four boys become stars on Broadway. She had so much to do with putting us there. Without her there would never have been the Marx Brothers. She was manipulative and intrusive and the stage mother of them all. She was also a great woman.

I still hear her voice as she talked to a family friend about us. "Sam can cough all night and I never hear him," she said. "But if one of my boys coughs just once, I'm wide awake."

150

Minnie's boys loved one another in the same way. Whenever a comedy team breaks up, the women who stand behind every man are usually the ones responsible. There was no way that could happen to us. We'd sooner shed the wives. I think that might have happened in a couple of cases.

Which brings me to another regret. I married three beautiful wrong women, just as they married the same wrong man. I need not amplify on that.

Though my memories are more crowded than most, and I often look back on yesterday, I choose to revel in today.

There's a prayer of sorts I recite to myself every night. I don't know where it comes from, but it's me: "Unborn tomorrow, and dead yesterday, why fret about them if today be sweet?"

The sentiment is so true. The yesterdays I cannot change even if I wanted to, and as for the tomorrows . . . I could take a walk next Thursday and get run over by a DeSoto.

Luck has walked with me all my life. It still does. The years have creaked up on me. I creaked back. It's not so easy to jump up and get a book any more. So I have it brought to me. Come to think of it, I'm not going to get up for any book, considering the quality of writing these days.

How lucky I have been to retain my faculties, for my mind to still be able to jump over tennis nets and to perform somersaults.

It's outrageous that my todays are so sweet. Everytime I complain that the sun isn't out, I think of Jack Benny, gone. He was a great comedian and one of the nicest men I ever knew.

A few months before he died, Jack was honored at a testimonial. "When we first met," I told the people assembled, "Jack was sixteen and I was nineteen. My mother wanted to put him in our act, but Jack's mother said he was too young to travel. Now he's eighty and I'm eighty-three. How time flies."

If, as a mutual friend put it, Jack died of an overdose of birthdays, what will he say about me?

151

This is what I can say about myself: I'm famous and healthy. Of the two, I'd rather be healthy. As my doctor says, there's nothing wrong with me . . . except mentally.

Ask Bob Hope and Milton Berle. A couple of years ago, a few of us old-timers were at some function where Lucille Ball was being honored.

"Lucy," I told her, "you're known for your beautiful legs. Could you show us one of them?"

She lifted her skirt a bit. I started to take off my clothes. Bob and Milton tried to stop me. They apparently thought I'd been overtaken by an attack of virility. All I wanted to do was to show them my Groucho T-shirt. I don't know why they should overreact to my actions, which are the same as they've always been.

They say a man is as old as the women he feels. In that case, I'm eighty-five.

I don't believe it for a moment, though it occasionally does remind me of my own mortality. Whatever happens, I want it known here and now that this is what I want on my tombstone: HERE LIES GROUCHO MARX, AND LIES AND LIES AND LIES. P.S. HE NEVER KISSED AN UGLY GIRL.

I think I'm going to kiss a good many pretty girls before I go. I suspect I'm going to live to a ripe old age.

APPENDIX

A Typical Audience Warm-Up
. . . Recorded August, 1952

GEORGE

Maybe we'd better rehearse it once . . . shall we?
"Here he is, the one, the only . . ."

AUDIENCE

Groucho!

GROUCHO

I like Ike.
(Audience applauds)

GROUCHO

Good evening, and welcome to *Dragnet.* I'm dragging and
my salary is net. Before we proceed with this show, I'd like to
introduce a few people who are responsible for making it a
failure. I'd like you to meet the director of the show
. . . Bob Dwan. Bob?
(Audience applauds)

BOB

Thank you. We thank you for—

GROUCHO

This is Bob Dwan, the director of the show.

BOB

Before we start—

GROUCHO

That'll give you an idea of the show.

BOB

We thank you for—

GROUCHO

He also meets trains at the Union Depot. If anybody has got

any relatives coming in downtown and you haven't got time to meet them, he'll be delighted to go down and escort them to any of the shabbier hotels. He used to be a hotel dick.

BOB

We're about ready to start now—

GROUCHO

I would hope so—

BOB

I would like to remind you—

GROUCHO

This is Mr. Dwan.

BOB

We, uh—

GROUCHO

Dwan also does dry cleaning, if there's anybody wants to get cleaned.

BOB

I would like to remind you—I'm sure most of you have seen the show. If you do, you'll notice perhaps that our quiz is a little different from most.

GROUCHO

Ours is crooked.

BOB

Well, beside that, we do have some rules, uhh, that we try to adhere to. We have tonight, I think, fifteen hundred dollars at stake between our couples—

GROUCHO

You can just about get a steak for fifteen hundred dollars.

BOB

And we in our quiz, unlike most other shows, we don't give any hints to our contestants—

GROUCHO

Unless we're related to them.

BOB

We attempt to keep—

GROUCHO

You're probably wondering why I took off that magnificent coat I was wearing and put this on, but only certain colors

will lend themselves to photography . . . and this happens to be one of the colors. There's a technical reason for this which unfortunately I can't explain, but Jimmy Van Trees, the head cameraman, he'll be delighted to come out here and clear the whole thing up. Jimmy, would you mind coming out here?
(Audience applauds)

GROUCHO

Jimmy just does this as a sideline. He was the cameraman on two of the movies we did over at RKO. That's why I'm not in the movie industry anymore. Really, he got weary of being at the studio every morning at seven o'clock. This is a sideline to him, he does this as a favor to us. He gets paid, but it's still a favor. Actually, his regular business—he has a chicken ranch at Tehachapi. It hasn't been doing very well, and I discovered why. He has three thousand roosters and one hen. You should see that hen around sundown. Kind of pathetic. This hen uses the excuse that women have been using since time immemorial—she says, "I've got a sick headache." It does fool some of the roosters, but not all of them. At any rate, this has nothing to do with what Jimmy was going to talk about. Would you mind explaining?

JIMMY

The concentric demands of the image—

GROUCHO

Now listen carefully to this. He also meets trains at the Union Depot.

JIMMY

The concentric demands of the image ortho— (next words muffled) when subject to equalizing (more muffled words) of the synchronizing generator . . . this is a radiant light flux, which modulates the electron beam, forcing the—

GROUCHO

Now are there any questions?
(Audience titters)

GROUCHO

Well, thanks, Jimmy. Now these kind of corrupt-looking faces that you see looming up above the fences here . . .

157

those are the assistant cameramen, and they all do mighty line and very important jobs. For which they get paid, so I don't know why I should stand here and apologize for them. And Mr. Dwan of course, despite a figure that keeps dashing in and out, is the director of the show. We also have musicians. We don't show them on television, on account of something about Petrillo-itis or something . . . they're pretty hammy. They like to be seen. Can we have the musicians come out here and take a bow, to show the audience that we actually have musicians, that they get paid?

> *JACK MEAKIN: We used to have this little laugh-getting device that we used for the warm-ups. Groucho would introduce the band, and what would happen was this: Each member would walk from the side curtain on one side of the stage over to the other. Once he was backstage, he'd run like hell to get to the other side. Heine Gunkler would start out. Then Buddy Collette would come out, then the other guys. When Heine came around the second time, nobody would pay much attention. But when Buddy came around the second time, the whole audience would go crazy, because Buddy is black, and they could then see that we were playing a joke on them. After they went around twice, they'd just continue going downstage to the orchestra pit.*

GROUCHO

They breed like rabbits, those musicians. Getting back to this coat, I'd like to digress for a second. You know, there are very few people that are familiar with high finance. I don't know how many of you know how many billion-dollar corporations there are in America. They're few and far between. There's AT&T, there's U.S. Steel (that was before Truman owned it). And, I don't know, a couple of others . . . Du Pont, and Standard Oil of New Jersey. Chrysler happens to be one of the billion-dollar corporations. Last year they had total sales of one billion three hundred million dollars, on which they had a profit after taxes of one hundred and sixty-five million dollars. And this is the coat they give me. This coat cost twenty-six dollars with seven pair of pants. Now, while I'm digressing, I'd like to bring up one

158

more subject, if we still have time here. There are all kinds of snobs in the world. You know, there are social snobs and financial snobs and family snobs and neighborhood snobs. And there are also joke snobs. That's a very strange thing. You can tell someone a joke, and if they've heard this joke, they point a finger at you accusingly, as if you were a criminal. They say, "I've heard that thing before." Now, there are wonderful jokes that are forty or fifty years old, that most of you people, who are comparatively young out here, I'm sure you haven't heard. For example, this is a real old joke. If you tell it to someone who's heard it, they get real angry. A fat woman walks into a drugstore and she says to the clerk, "I'd like to have some chafing powder." The druggist says, "Walk this way." She says, "If I could walk that way, I wouldn't need the powder."

(Audience laughs)

GROUCHO

Now, you see, that's a real old joke, but you all enjoyed it and a very few of you had heard it . . . which reminds me of my kid. I have a little girl five years old, and she goes to kindergarten in Westwood. Frequently I pick her up after school and take her home. The other day I said to her, "Melinda, what do you do in this school? You never tell me anything about this school. What do you do all day from nine to three?" She said, "All we do is paint and go to the terlet."

Well, at any rate, these are the musicians over here. You've seen them before. Could we have some music just so that we can convince the customers that you can actually play? What about the trumpet?

(Trumpet plays racing theme)

That'll give you an idea of the kind of life he leads. Luckily, he'll soon be drafted and we won't have to worry about him. Now what about the trombone?

(Trombone plays "Too Young")

He's one of the original Sons of the Pioneers. That'll give you an idea of how difficult it was to have children in those cov-

ered wagons. What about the clarinet?
(*Clarinet plays "I Get Ideas"*)

What is that?

AUDIENCE

I get ideas.

GROUCHO

What is it?

AUDIENCE

I get ideas.

GROUCHO

You ought to be ashamed of yourself!
(*Audience laughs*)
How you get sucked into that every week. You'll never learn.
The bull fiddle.
(*Bull fiddle plays scales*)
Believe me he needs every minute of it too. And now the
drums?
(*Drum player goes wild*)
Now you know what a steady diet of marijuana will do for a
drummer.

I see some servicemen out front tonight. What branch of
the service are you in?

AIRMEN

(Their answer is muffled)

GROUCHO

What is it?

AIRMEN

Air Force!

GROUCHO

Oh . . . I thought you were letter carriers. Any others from
the Air Force tonight? Stand up . . . come on . . . stand
up. A little Air Force music, boys.
(*Band plays "Wild Blue Yonder"*)
(*Procedure is repeated with Army, Navy, Marine songs*)

GROUCHO

For the first time in the history of this war, we're really getting someplace. I see this morning they fired a general. Where are the Marines?

MARINES

Over here!

GROUCHO

What do you hear from Harry?
(*Theme is played*)

GROUCHO

Anybody here from the Coast Guard?
(*No answer*)

GROUCHO

I have a son here who was in the last war in the Coast Guard. Stand up and we'll hear a little Coast Guard music. Come on, on your feet.
(*Audience applauds as Arthur stands*)
Pathetic . . . they don't even have a song, the Coast Guard. They were so busy getting drunk they didn't have time to write one. Well, now a little civilian music for the deserters in the audience.
(*Band plays*)
And Mr. Dwan of course you've met, this is the director of the show.

BOB

I would like to remind you again about the rules of our quiz. It's important to our—

GROUCHO

There's a girl out there with a loose sweater. I wish there was a loose girl out there with a tight sweater. I'd certainly like to pull the wool over *her* eyes. The audiences are getting increasingly filthier each week. I guess it's spring. Now, Mr. Dwan of course you've met.
(*Groucho sings "Omaha, Nebraska"*)

BOB

Briefly, about the rules of our game, if we hear any answers to the questions from the audience, we're required to throw that question out and substitute another which is often more difficult than the first one. We try to give each couple an

161

equal break, in other words, and we simply can't allow any help from the audience. I'm sure you'll understand as we play the game. We would like also to have your picture as part of our show, but instead of putting these bright lights on you all through the show, if you would stay for about fifteen seconds afterwards, we'll turn the cameras around and you will then be able to wave back at yourselves on the screens all over the country when the picture is finally released. Now that's about— (*Bob never gets a chance to finish—the show has started*)

GEORGE

Ladies and gentlemen—the secret word tonight is "floor." F-L-Double-O-R.

GROUCHO

Rally?

GEORGE

You bet your life!
(*Theme music comes on*)

GEORGE

The more than three thousand De Soto-Ply. ¬outh Dealers of America present Groucho Marx in *You Bet Your Life,* the comedy quiz series produced and transcribed in Hollywood. Now here he is, the one, the only—

AUDIENCE

GROUCHO!

A Compendium Of Groucho One-Liners

To a Western Union employee:
   Do you still charge for a Stop?—like I know what you're doing in Atlantic City Stop!

To a Maid of Cotton:
   Cotton is very important, Pat. How else could they sell silk shirts for three and a half dollars?

To a pretty girl:
   You have a very good head on your shoulders, and I wish it were on mine.

To a watchmaker:
   Where's your business—on the main stem?

To Melba Taylor:
   You're Melba Taylor? You must be the toast of the town!

To Chief Nino Cochise of the Apache Tribe:
   Chief, I'm glad to meet you. You're not the chief that runs from here to Chicago in thirty-nine hours, huh?

To a cartoonist:
   If you want to see a comic strip, you should see me in a shower.

To a father of triplets:
　You've been married fifteen months and you have three daughters? This is indeed the age of rapid transit.

To a baseball umpire:
　And do you have any little thieves at home?

To a dealer in war surplus:
　How many times have you been indicted?

To a dress designer who said women dress for themselves, not for men:
　If they dressed for me, the stores wouldn't sell much—just an occasional sun visor.

To a meteorologist:
　Any little squalls at home running around with their barometers dropping?

To a pharmacist:
　Is it true that Rexall is a drug on the market?

To a professional gambler:
　Have you ever had an unusual experience—like letting a customer win once in a while?

To a tree surgeon:
　Have you ever fallen out of a patient?

To a sky-writer:
　When you're up there sky-writing do you ever feel that someone is looking over your shoulder?

To a pretty schoolteacher:
　How would you like to take over my student body?

To elderly newlyweds:
I'll never forget my wedding day . . . they threw vitamin pills.

To an admiral:
We're not very formal on the show, so do you mind if I call you Captain?

To a marriage broker:
I met my wife on a ferry boat, and when we landed she gave me the slip.

To Gary Cooper's mother:
He's a real chatterbox too . . . I've been watching him for twenty years in the movies and I would say conversationally, he's about six words ahead of my brother Harpo.

To Fred Haney, manager of the Milwaukee Braves:
This is the man who made Milwaukee famous, you know. He also made Milwaukee come in second—or was it third?

To a male contestant:
So your name is John Rose—that's a simple declarative, isn't it?

To a musician:
Beethoven is famous for his fifth, and he never touched a drop.

To Father Reagan:
What kind of business are you in?

To Bobby Van:
I know Bobby Van. You moved me into my house . . . Bobby Van and Storage.

To a pretty girl:
You're quite a dish, Marie, and since I'm the head dish around here, let's start cooking.

To a muscleman:
You don't have any muscles unless you take your jacket off, and I don't have any muscles until I put my jacket on.

To an English teacher:
I thought homonym was a cereal.

To an Irishman:
Some of my best friends are Irish . . . like Harry McRuby and David O'Selznick.

To a Vassar graduate:
Were you fat when you left Vassar or did you leave Vassar-lean?

To an author:
It won't do you any good to plug your book on my show, because none of our listeners can read.

To a housewife:
Your husband has a very good head for business, and if you take my advice you'll have it examined the first thing in the morning.

To a poet:
In other words you're out of work?

To a war veteran:
Well, that's highly commendable . . . I knew his brother, Haile Selassie.

To a police officer:
You have nothing on me, copper, I've been busy every

night this week at meetings of the Beverly Hills Mafia.

To a chicken raiser:
   How many did you raise and how high did you raise them?

To two Heidis:
   I'll call you Heidi-Hi . . . and I'll call you Heidi-Ho . . .
and you can call me Cab Calloway.

To a fat woman:
   I bet you're a lot of fun at a party . . . in fact you *are* a
party.

To the singing Marks Brothers:
   Boys, if you ever get the desire to sing again, please call
yourselves the McGuire Sisters.

To a champion diver:
   I've been reading about your feats on the diving board for
years . . . you did have your feets on the diving board?

To a cook:
   I tried boiling pig's feet once, but I couldn't get the pig to
stand still.

To a Swiss man:
   Switzerland is a wonderful country . . . everyone seems
so friendly . . . particularly when they clip the tourists.

To the owner of a 1902 auto:
   You must have it paid by this time.

To a Chinese punster:
   You know, you're a bigger menace than the Asiatic flu.

To Dr. Howard Drum:
   Well, if you're a drum, you can beat it anytime, Doc.

To a dentist:
I *thought* you looked down in the mouth.

To a Scottish girl:
Whether you're straight scotch or not, I'd like to be your chaser.

To a choreographer:
Oh, you make maps?

To a native of Canton:
I had that for dinner last night—canned tongue.

To Global Zobel:
Global Zobel—that's quite euphonious . . . it's one of the euphonious names I've ever heard.

To a contestant:
You say a buffoon is a clown?—I thought a buffoon is like an aspirin except that it works faster.

To an economist:
I made a killing on Wall Street a few years ago . . . I shot my broker.

To a Superior Court bailiff:
That's a good job, especially if you like to sleep in the daytime.

Brief Exchanges

GROUCHO: Do your parents live in L.A.?

CURVY GIRL: Yes, they do. My father is a meat distributor here.

GROUCHO: Your father is a meat distributor? Well, if you're any indication, he certainly knows his business.

GROUCHO: A walking race? I've never seen a walking race, with the exception of a couple of horses I bet on at Santa Anita. Well, how would a walker do against a horse?

MAN: Well, in one hundred yards, I beat a horse, and I beat a car with a twenty-five-yard handicap.

GROUCHO: Well, that's understandable. How fast can a horse drive an automobile? It'll take ten thousand dollars to sponsor you to walk across the country?

MAN: Ten thousand dollars.

GROUCHO: Here's a buck. I'm sponsoring you as far as Hollywood and Vine. From there on, you'll have to take a bus.

GROUCHO: Where do you do your teaching, Jody?

JODY: I teach for Meglin's.

GROUCHO: You teach meglins? What are meglins?

JODY: The famous Meglin Kiddies?

GROUCHO: Oh, Meglin Kiddies. Isn't that the one that teaches precocious children to become dancers and actors?

JODY: Oh, we have lots of wonderful children in our school.

GROUCHO: It's on Obnoxious Boulevard, isn't it?

GROUCHO: Is your wife of Italian extraction too?

MAN: No, she's a Slav, Groucho.

GROUCHO: Well, I'm sorry to hear that. I'm sure with a little patience you can teach her to be neater.

FENNEMAN: Groucho, we have a couple of special guests with us—

GROUCHO: Mr. Marx, if you please. Do I call *you* Groucho?

GROUCHO: Would you like to join me for moon-gazing some night, when there isn't any moon?

PENNY: Well, thank you, but I'm very happily married.

GROUCHO: Oh. I was just checking, Penny, that's all. I was just curious to know how far a Penny will go these days. And it went about as far as I thought it would. You look pretty young to be married. Why did you tie the knot? Was he a Penny pincher?

PENNY: No, it was love at first sight. And we've been married for four years.

GROUCHO: Well, why was it love at first sight? Was he wearing his wallet outside of his pocket?

GROUCHO: You gonna stand on your head now?

MAN: Well, I'm gonna need a little room,

GROUCHO: We'll get you a little room right after the show.

GROUCHO: Where are you from, Frankie?

FRANKIE: Brown Military Academy, sir.

GROUCHO: You were born in a military academy?

FRANKIE: No, sir.

GROUCHO: How did you arrive? Were you shot out of a cannon?

GROUCHO: Where's your home, Marie?

MARIE: Memphis, Tennessee. Way down in Dixie.

GROUCHO: Well, that's mighty fine country around there.

MARIE: Certainly is.

170

GROUCHO: Got a lot of cornpone around there.

MARIE: Oh, you bet! Ham hocks and navy beans—

GROUCHO: Yes. A ham hock—that's an actor that puts his watch in soak.

PILOT: I'm a helicopter pilot.

GROUCHO: Say, you certainly have an appropriate name for it—Eagle. That's certainly a good name for a helicopter pilot. But don't mention it quite so loud—because there are children listening. Say heck-i-copter. No, we try to be that way on this show. Every once in a while the Nice Nellie comes out in me. Tell me, what's the difference between a helicopter pilot and a regular orthodox pilot?

PILOT: Well, a helicopter pilot pilots helicopters and—

GROUCHO: I'm going to get some great answers from you.

PILOT:—and a regular pilot pilots airplanes.

GROUCHO: Well, I have a pilot in my gas stove, and it doesn't pilot anything. It's out most of the time, and so am I. I'm home on the range occasionally.

WOMAN: When a boy kisses a girl and she says "Stop," usually she means, "Stop it. I love it." And it was sort of like that.

GROUCHO: You mean when a girl says "Stop," she really means "Don't stop"? Boy, the nights I've wasted. I was always so gullible.

GROUCHO: You mean when you were a young buck you traveled all the way from Washington to Arizona on horseback?

MAN: That's right.

GROUCHO: Couldn't do it today, Chief. The buck today doesn't go nearly as far as it used to.

GROUCHO: Now, Sandy, where did you meet Dolores?

SANDY: Well, a couple of years ago we worked at NBC in Portland.

GROUCHO: You worked at NBC in Portland? Well, that's a

171

wonderful network, NBC, and I'm glad you have us in Portland. Portland! I salute you. NBC has another affiliate. What station does NBC have in Portland?

SANDY: It wasn't a station. It was the National Biscuit Company.

MAN: I can tell you one (joke) that I gave an act. When they were a little short, because another act was on the same show that used some of their gags.

GROUCHO: What do you mean the act was short? Was this Singer's Midgets?

MAN: My brother and I own a business called Up and Atom.

GROUCHO: Well, what is it? A breakfast cereal with fallout?

FENNEMAN: Well, Groucho, we've invited some railroad men to be on our show tonight.

GROUCHO: Do you keep track of them yourself? That's the tie that binds.

GROUCHO: How old are you, Jean?

JEAN: I generally say I'm one year older than Jack Benny.

GROUCHO: You mean you're ninety-seven? You don't look it.

GROUCHO: You say you have patterns that will allow me to build anything I want?

WOMAN: Yes.

GROUCHO: Well, can you send me the pattern to Anita Ekberg?

GROUCHO: Tell me, Rabbi. Do you get many actors at your temple?

RABBI: Yes, quite a few.

GROUCHO: I'm surprised you allow so much ham in your temple.

GROUCHO: What's the "F" in your name stand for?
MAN: Ferdinand.
GROUCHO: Ferdinand? Well, bully for you.

GROUCHO: You look pretty shifty to me. What sort of racket are you in?
MAN: Well, I build and wreck homes.
GROUCHO: You wreck homes? Are you the editor of one of those scandal magazines?

GROUCHO: Could you give me some idea of your age, Jeanne?
JEANNE: Groucho, that's something I don't even admit to my husband.
GROUCHO: Jeannie, if you've got a husband, I've lost interest in your age, anyway.

GROUCHO: Well, John, I've been studying you, and I think I can call your occupation. Are you an undertaker?
JOHN: No, sir, I'm a farmer.
GROUCHO: Well, farmer . . . undertaker . . . what's the difference? You're both planters.

GROUCHO: Are you interested in marriage?
GIRL: I'm a woman, aren't I?
GROUCHO: Well, even with these glasses I didn't think you were Sonny Tufts.

GROUCHO: Rock and Roll is springing up in Japan?
WOMAN: Yes.
GROUCHO: That'll teach them to send us the Asiatic Flu.

WOMAN: I have two locks of Elvis Presley's hair.
GROUCHO: Do you have any cream cheese to go with it?

GROUCHO: Let's see. You're Walter Knott?
KNOTT: Yes, I'm Knott.

173

GROUCHO: You're a Knott, did you say?

KNOTT: Knott, yes.

GROUCHO: Well, we're making pretty good time. We're making three knots an hour . . . and you say you've been married forty-three years?

KNOTT: That's right.

GROUCHO: You're the kind of knot that doesn't come untied.

GROUCHO: Whereabouts in Manhattan were you born?

WOMAN: On Riverside Drive.

GROUCHO: Oh, well. You're lucky you weren't run over by a bus.

GROUCHO: You say you write for papers all over the world?

WOMAN: Yes.

GROUCHO: And do they send them to you?

GROUCHO: Where did you get the name Crash? Was your father a stockbroker or were you born on the freeway?

CRASH CORRIGAN: No, Groucho, I was making action pictures, and of course I did some football playing. The way I used to tackle somebody, instead of fighting with them with my fists, I used to take off and dive at them headfirst. And that's how I got the name Crash.

GROUCHO: Well, I'm glad they don't name all the actors by the way they fight. Otherwise I'd be known as Kick-Them-in-the-Shins-and-Run-Like-the-Devil Marx.

GROUCHO: What's your name?

MAN: Boyd.

GROUCHO: Why don't you have a beard, then you could be a Boyd in the bush?

MAN: I lived with cannibals in the jungle.

GROUCHO: You're lucky you didn't go to pot.

174

WOMAN: I have woodpeckers in my cocoa palms.
GROUCHO: You have woodpeckers in your cocoa palms?
WOMAN: That's right.
GROUCHO: Well, keep your hat on and nobody will notice.

WOMAN: Have you ever milked a soybean, Groucho?
GROUCHO: Milked a soybean?
WOMAN: Yes.
GROUCHO: I'd like to, but how do you get under it?

GROUCHO: What are your duties these days with the Air Force?
MAN: I'm commander of the 146th Fighter Interceptor Wing of the California Air National Guard.
GROUCHO: What does California need an Air Force for? We have no air out here.

MAN: I'm a blood analyst.
GROUCHO: Well, don't look at me unless you analyze Geritol.

GROUCHO: How many times have you been bitten by a dog?
WOMAN: Just once in the last four years.
GROUCHO: That's a pretty good record. Where'd he bite you?
WOMAN: In Encino.
GROUCHO: Why, that dirty mongrel!

GROUCHO: When did you leave Chicago?
WOMAN: When I was a little child.
GROUCHO: And where did you grow up?
WOMAN: Chico.
GROUCHO: I grew up around Chico myself. You don't happen to be Gummo, do you?

GROUCHO: How old are you, Edy?
WOMAN: Oh, a gentleman never asks a woman her age.
GROUCHO: That's right. How old are you?

GROUCHO: Did you ever hear of a cow that just gives buttermilk?
MAN: No.
GROUCHO: What else can a cow give *but her milk?*

GROUCHO: What's your name?
SHIRLEY: Shirley.
GROUCHO: Well, Shirley to bed, and Shirley to rise.

GROUCHO: Have you ever kissed the Blarney Stone?
MAN: Yes, I have.
GROUCHO: Well, how does it compare with your wife?
MAN: Well, the Blarney Stone is supposed to give you the power of speech. When I kiss my wife, I'm speechless.

GROUCHO: That's pretty poetic, isn't it? The sea of matrimony?
WOMAN: Yes.
GROUCHO: That means you usually get sunk as soon as you leave the pulpit.

GROUCHO: Where do you go on your nights out?
WOMAN: Well, I go to showers and to—
GROUCHO: Can't you take a shower at home?

MAN: I'm from Rising Sun.
GROUCHO: I have a rising son. His name is Arthur and he usually rises around two in the afternoon.

WOMAN: After we were married, my husband enlisted in the Air Force and we traveled around for four more years.
GROUCHO: Did you ever settle down long enough to raise a family?

176

WOMAN: Well, no, but I had one. My children were born from one end of the country to the other.

GROUCHO: You must have pretty long children.

GROUCHO: You look like a very wealthy and successful confidence man.

MAN: Thank you.

GROUCHO: What is it like in South Carolina?

WOMAN: Oh, it's wonderful, Groucho. Southern hospitality and wonderful folks.

GROUCHO: Well, we want you to feel at home here, Marie, so we'll pay you off in Confederate money.

GROUCHO: How did you meet your wife?

MAN: A friend of mine.

GROUCHO: Do you still regard him as a friend?

GROUCHO: Here I am again . . . all shaken up from a very harrowing experience.

FENNEMAN: Oh, really? What happened?

GROUCHO: It was terrible. I had a puncture. First one I've had in years. I ran over a whiskey bottle on the highway.

FENNEMAN: Couldn't you see the whiskey bottle?

GROUCHO: How could I see it? It was in a pedestrian's back pocket . . . He wasn't killed though. It was eighty-six proof.

GROUCHO: Well, Beverly, tell me, have you been looking for a husband?

BEVERLY: Well, not looking, but I keep my eyes open.

GROUCHO: Are you sure you've looked in the right places, Beverly? How about where you work? What kind of work have you done?

BEVERLY: Well, I've been in the Marine Corps for the last three years until recently.

GROUCHO: And you couldn't find a man in the Marine Corps?

BEVERLY: No, I couldn't.

GROUCHO: Well, the Marines aren't landing like they used to.

GROUCHO: I don't know much about French menus. Suppose I came into your restaurant. What should I order?

MAN: You just ask for me.

GROUCHO: Are *you* on the menu?

GROUCHO: What does a girl think when she meets a handsome boy?

COED: Oh, I imagine she thinks about the same thing boys do.

GROUCHO: You mean girls too wonder if they'll be drafted?

GROUCHO: You don't mind if I ask you a few personal questions, do you?

MODEL: If they're not too embarrassing.

GROUCHO: Don't give it a second thought. I've asked thousands of questions on this show and I've yet to be embarrassed.

GROUCHO: What were people wearing when you were a baby?

Elderly WOMAN: Diapers.

GROUCHO: Where did you meet your wife?

MAN: In my delicatessen.

GROUCHO: Was she pickled at the time?

PRETTY GIRL: I'm afraid you don't follow me.

GROUCHO: Even if I did, you'd have nothing to be afraid of. (*To male contestant*) Can you follow her?

MALE: Yes.

GROUCHO: Does your wife know you go around following strange women?

LADY ANALYST: Tell me what's wrong with this sentence: Him and her went to the movies.

GROUCHO: It should be her and him. Ladies first, you know. Now tell me, what was your analysis? What job am I suited for?

LADY ANALYST: Only what you're doing now.

GROUCHO: Are you interested in matrimony?

FAN CLUB PRESIDENT: Indeed I am.

GROUCHO: Do you have any other interests?

FAN CLUB PRESIDENT: You haven't mentioned Elvis Presley.

GROUCHO: I seldom do unless I stub my toe.

GROUCHO: Is this your sister or your wife?

MAN: My wife, Groucho.

GROUCHO: Well, just checking. You know the old saying. An ounce of prevention is worth a pound of bandages and adhesive tape.

GROUCHO: How long have you been married?

WOMAN: Two and a half years, Groucho.

GROUCHO: Why are you holding on to each other? Are you afraid if you let go, you'll kill each other?

GROUCHO: How long have you been married?

WOMAN: Three wonderful years.

GROUCHO: Never mind the wonderful years. How many miserable years have you had?

GROUCHO: Do you have a job?

FATHER OF TRIPLETS: Yes.

GROUCHO: What is it?

FATHER OF TRIPLETS: I work for the California Power Company.

GROUCHO: My boy, you don't work for the California Power Company. You *are* the California Power Company.

GROUCHO: How long have you been married, Bill?

BILL: Fourteen years.

GROUCHO: Fourteen years? You've had the seven-year itch twice?

GROUCHO: How did you get to be a headwaiter, Felix? Did you start out as an ordinary burglar?

FELIX: No, I started in New York as a waiter many years ago.

GROUCHO: Well, it's a very honorable profession. I was just being facetious. What distinguishes a waiter from a head-waiter, Felix?

FELIX: Well, it depends on a lot of circumstances. And of course personality has a lot to do with it.

GROUCHO: That's right. To be a headwaiter you have to have something wrong with your personality. I'd take my hat off to you, Felix, except that it would cost me two bits to get it back.

GROUCHO: You're in the luau business? What do you do? You cater these things?

MAX: Yes.

GROUCHO: Well, suppose I wanted to throw one of these nightmares. What's the first thing I have to do—steal a bana-na tree?

MAX: No. First thing I do is go into the backyard of your house to look over the grounds.

GROUCHO: Why do you have to look over my grounds in the back of the house?

MAX: So I can dig a five-foot hole.

GROUCHO: Max, if your food's that bad, you'll have to find someplace else to bury it.

GROUCHO: You know how to make a Venetian blind?

MAN: No.

GROUCHO: Get him drunk. That's the best way.

MAN: I'd rather be a cattleman than a banker, 'cause after all, a banker, you know, bankers never die, they just lose interest.

GROUCHO: Not the bankers I know. They'd rather die than lose any interest.

GROUCHO: What is a fur factory? I thought a live mink was the only fur factory there was.

MAN: After the mink gets through making the mink, we skin them and make them into various garments, for beauty as well as for warmth.

GROUCHO: I see. First you skin the mink and then you skin the customers.

MAN: We don't skin the customers.

GROUCHO: That's when the fur really flies.

WIFE: I spoil my husband rotten.

GROUCHO: You spoil him? Then why don't you shove him in the freezer? That'll keep him from spoiling.

GROUCHO: What's your husband's name?

WOMAN: Milton August.

GROUCHO: What's his name in September?

GROUCHO: Where are you from?

WOMAN: I'm from South Wales.

GROUCHO: Did you ever meet a fellow named Jonah? He lived in whales for a while. The middle part.

WOMAN: My father was a rear admiral in the Royal Navy.

GROUCHO: A rear admiral? You mean you never saw his face?

GROUCHO: What are you planning to do after college?

STUDENT: Be a lawyer.

GROUCHO: A lawyer. I see. Are you planning to go into politics or go straight?

GROUCHO: Would you be interested in Carol here?

RAUL: Very much so, but unfortunately I have a girl in Rio.

GROUCHO: You mean you prefer a girl who's five thousand miles away to a girl who's standing right next to you?

RAUL: Well, I'm very faithful.

GROUCHO: There are more nuts in Brazil than I suspected.

GROUCHO: Your husband is twenty, and the youngest commercial pilot in the world? How can he fly those big planes, Tootsie?

TOOTSIE: Well, he has lots of experience.

GROUCHO: So have I, but I still get dizzy . . . I get dizzy climbing up on a stool at a soda fountain. Although I was a stool pigeon for years.

GIRL: I would say it's what's upstairs that counts.

GROUCHO: Well, I have something upstairs. My upstairs maid. And that's not easy because I only have a one-story house. And the one story you're not going to hear is about my upstairs maid.

GROUCHO: Now did you always want to be a singer?

JOHN CHARLES THOMAS: No. As I said a moment ago, I always wanted to be a surgeon.

GROUCHO: Oh, a surgeon.

JOHN CHARLES THOMAS: And I matriculated into Mount Street School of Homeopathy in Baltimore.

GROUCHO: Oh—well, I should think medicine and voice would go very well together. You could operate on a patient and then pick up another couple of bucks singing at the funeral.

GROUCHO: Is your wife listening?

MAN: Well no . . . I don't know. She may be. But she don't like comedians, Groucho, so she may not be listening.

GROUCHO: Well, if she doesn't like comedians, there's no reason why she shouldn't watch this show.

GROUCHO: Where are you learning to be a barber? Do you go to school?

WOMAN: Yes. I go to the American Barber College.

GROUCHO: The Barber College? Must have some pretty gay blades there.

MAN: She kicked me under the table.

GROUCHO: She kicked you under the table? And did you remain there?

GROUCHO: How many times have you made a parachute jump?

WOMAN: Eleven hundred.

GROUCHO: You landed eleven hundred times?

WOMAN: That's right.

GROUCHO: No wonder you're only five feet tall. Every time you grew an inch you pounded it right back in again.

GROUCHO: Is your perfume expensive, Eddie? If it is, perhaps that's why I haven't heard of it. How much do you charge for a gallon of this stuff? Or can you buy it on draught?

MAN: No, you can't buy it on draught, but the price runs from three dollars for a purse size in Arpege, up to five hundred dollars for thirty-two ounces.

GROUCHO: Thirty-two ounces? Is that a gallon?

MAN: No, a quart.

GROUCHO: Five hundred dollars a quart?

MAN: Five hundred dollars a quart for Arpege.

GROUCHO: Well, do they get a nickel back when they return the bottle? Are there really any husbands who are willing to shell out five hundred dollars for a bottle of perfume for their wives?

MAN: Not for their wives.

GROUCHO: You don't have to explain that. I've been around. I'll bet you certainly look forward to Mother's Day.

GROUCHO: What made you decide to live in Azusa—as opposed to Paris or London?

183

GROUCHO: What makes a plane stay up in the air? I've never been able to figure it out.

WOMAN: The lift from the air holds the wing up. Air is very dense.

GROUCHO: What was that last thing? The air is what?

WOMAN: Dense.

GROUCHO: Well, I'd love to! Do you care to waltz or rhumba?

GROUCHO: Have you ever done any flying, Johnny?

MAN: Yes, Groucho, a little. I had about forty-five minutes of a stick and I was also a stunt man on old Jenny.

GROUCHO: Really, did you know old Jenny?

MAN: Jenny airplane, Groucho.

GROUCHO: I've done many a stunt with old Jenny. And we had a high time together.

GROUCHO: Say, you two'd make a great team. What's your opinion, Nick?

MAN: I think she's real gone.

GROUCHO: No, she's still here. But what's your opinion?

GROUCHO: He'll keep on sending flowers after he's married. All married men do that, you know. And if you're lucky, on your birthday he might even remember to send some to you.

FENNEMAN: Some special guests are ready to meet you now. As a matter of fact, when I heard about them, I asked them to do something we don't ordinarily do on the show—

GROUCHO: What's that? Be amusing?

MAN: We've only had one other child born to a governor and his wife while in office.

GROUCHO: Well, that is unusual. I've never seen a stork flying over the governor's mansion.

MAN: Well, uh—

GROUCHO: I've seen a lot of vultures hanging around there.

MAN: I have found the glamor is truly glamor, and that these stars are truly wonderful people. They are like your neighbor next door, really.

GROUCHO: Well, answer one question. Are there any houses for rent in your neighborhood?

WOMAN: I just arrived from Phoenix about a month ago and—

GROUCHO: Felix? The cat?

WOMAN: No, from Phoenix, and I haven't met any yet.

GROUCHO: You haven't met any? How long have you been here?

WOMAN: About a month.

GROUCHO: You've been here a month and you haven't met anybody yet?

WOMAN: No.

GROUCHO: Well, where have you been spending your time? Forest Lawn?

WOMAN: Well, I know what I'd like to be.

GROUCHO: What would you like to be, honey?

WOMAN: A race car driver.

GROUCHO: A race car driver. There's the way it goes— here's a girl who's perfect for parking, and all she wants to do is racing.

MAN: Oh, it's right on the edge of my tongue.

GROUCHO: Well, stick your tongue out.

GROUCHO: What are you gonna do with your money, Colonel?

MAN: I'm gonna make my wife happy, Groucho.

GROUCHO: What are you gonna do—get a divorce?

GROUCHO: For those who don't know, a baby-sitter is someone who gets seventy-five cents an hour for watching television and cleaning out your icebox.

GROUCHO: (To Ray Bradbury) What kind of a job do you have, Ray?

RAY: I'm a writer.

GROUCHO: What kind of a rider? Pony Express, motorcycle, or what?

RAY: *Writer.* W-R-I-T-E-R.

GROUCHO: Oh, that's very refreshing—a writer who can spell.

GROUCHO: (To a bell ringer) Was you wife with you all this time?

MAN: No, I never married.

GROUCHO: Well that's a shame. You've been interested in the wrong kind of bells. You should go down to the beach some time when the belles are peeling. You know, I had to leave town one time because of a belle at Santa Monica. This was one of the belles that told at midnight. She told the police.

GROUCHO: Now where are you from? Are you from Pasadena?

MAN: I was born right here.

GROUCHO: Right here in the studio? I realize that you've been standing there for quite some time, but I didn't think it was that long.

MAN: Well, I've traveled in a great many countries in the foreign service of the government doing personnel work, but Los Angeles is the most wonderful place in the world to live.

GROUCHO: Well, I agree, it's a wonderful city, even though I do criticize it occasionally. I'm all for it. And if they'd lower the taxes and get rid of the smog and clean up the traffic mess, I really believe I'd settle here until the next earthquake.

186

MAN: You can't get an ant to go straight.
GROUCHO: That's been true of a number of mine.

GROUCHO: Jack and Jill are your kids' names? Well, what is your wife's name? Mother Goose?

GROUCHO: Where is your office, Doc?
MAN: In Wilmington, Groucho, in the Los Angeles Harbor.
GROUCHO: Oh well, that's the place for a dock—down in the harbor.

GROUCHO: You say it was a Tennessee walking horse?
MAN: Yes, sir.
GROUCHO: Is that the fellow who wrote "Cat on a Hot Tin Roof"?

MAN: I'm what you call a horse psychiatrist.
GROUCHO: A horse psychiatrist?
MAN: Right.
GROUCHO: You must have the biggest couch in town. I suppose you get a lot of horses whose wives are nags?

GROUCHO: (To Liberace) Lib, we're glad to have you here.
LIBERACE: Well, it's a pleasure.
GROUCHO: You don't object to me calling you Lib, huh?
LIBERACE: Not at all.
GROUCHO: Matter of fact, I'm a prominent member of the Liberace Fan Club.
LIBERACE: Well, that's wonderful.
GROUCHO: Last year I was voted Chief Candle Snuffer.

GROUCHO: Where you from, Lil?
WOMAN: I'm from Iran.
GROUCHO: Oh, I thought you were from Kansas City. Iran, isn't that where Great Britain had some trouble about oil concessions not long ago?
WOMAN: Yes.

187

GROUCHO: Well Britain can keep their oil. You're the one I want some concessions from.

GROUCHO: Do you have any particular steady boyfriend?
WOMAN: Yes, I do.
GROUCHO: Or do you have a boy friend who *isn't* particularly steady?

GROUCHO: What's your name?
WOMAN: Mimi Pill.
GROUCHO: Mimi Pill? I find that pretty hard to swallow. Imagine finding a pill like this in your aspirin bottle.

WOMAN: I like American food very much.
GROUCHO: Well, kid, I'm your meat.

GROUCHO: Are you married, Bill?
BILL: No, I'm separated.
GROUCHO: When a man gets to be your age, you have to expect to start coming apart. Maybe you've been using the wrong kind of glue.

GROUCHO: What's your name?
MAN: Mr. Cummings.
GROUCHO: Are you cummings through the rye?

GROUCHO: Have you ever been injured riding a motorcycle?
WOMAN: Many times.
GROUCHO: You have, huh? Well, they're not evident, these injuries. You look pretty healthy. Do you have any scars to prove it?
WOMAN: All over me.
GROUCHO: You have, huh? What do you mean, all over you? Specifically, where did you get these scars?
WOMAN: Well, let's see. Some of 'em were in Santa Monica, North Hollywood, and—

GROUCHO: Listen, when I want a lesson in geography, I'll speak to Rand McNally.

MAN: I was born in Brisbane, Australia.
GROUCHO: Australia, eh? You have more of an American accent than an Australian accent.
MAN: Well, there is a distinct accent, I suppose. For example, what you call a bison is a buffalo, and what we call a bison is a place where an Australian washes his face.
GROUCHO: Well, I've washed my face in Buffalo, when I was playing up there.

GROUCHO: What do you do?
WOMAN: I'm a dance instructor for Arthur Murray.
GROUCHO: You mean after all these years Arthur still hasn't learned how to dance?

MAN: I'm from County Cork.
GROUCHO: That explains why you bobbed up here.

GROUCHO: Do you manufacture beach umbrellas?
MAN: No.
GROUCHO: Awnings?
MAN: No.
GROUCHO: Venetian blinds?
MAN: No, Groucho.
GROUCHO: In that case, I apologize. I was sure you were mixed up in something shady, but what kind of a racket are you in?
MAN: At present, I'm involved in the motion picture business.
GROUCHO: Well, that's a pretty good racket. Have you produced any pictures?
MAN: Yes, one picture.
GROUCHO: You're a producer, huh? Bill Hunter. I think I saw your picture.
MAN: Oh?
GROUCHO: It was hanging on the wall in the Post Office.

GROUCHO: Mrs. Smith, are you in business by yourself, or are you connected with a law firm?

WOMAN: Well, I'm with Mordel, Mordel, Mordel and Smith.

GROUCHO: If you were smart, you'd get yourself a good lawyer and get out of that. Why is your name on the end?

WOMAN: I was the last one in.

GROUCHO: What, were you racing to the office?

WOMAN: I think when Philadelphia lawyers prepare a brief, their briefs are probably fifty pages long, and a brief that we would make here would be about five pages long.

GROUCHO: Well, you must remember that Philadelphia has a much colder climate and you need longer briefs there than you do here.

MAN: I did have a pretty good record before coming to Stanford.

GROUCHO: What—with the police?

GROUCHO: Imagine. Frankie Anvalo . . . Avalon on my show. Now I'm all aflutter. I can't even pronounce his name correctly. You know, it isn't every week that we get a famous celebrity up here, and I want to tell you, this is one of the biggest moments in the history of this show. This'll give you an idea of the show.

AVALON: We have four girls in Philadelphia who take care of the fan club, and four girls in New York who—that's all they do is just take care of the fan club.

GROUCHO: You have eight girls who do nothing but answer your mail?

AVALON: Right.

GROUCHO: Your staff is bigger than my fan club.

GROUCHO: Well how do you explain so many singers coming from one section of the city (Philly)? Is it because they don't produce any ballplayers there?

190

AVALON: I'll tell you what. Y'know, before, mothers used to meet on the street and they used to say uh, "How's your son doing?" and they'd say, "Fine." But now they meet on the streets and they say, "How's your son's record doing?" 'Cause everybody's recording in South Philadelphia.

GROUCHO: Well, it was like that where I came from. My mother would say to another, "How's your son's record?"

WOMAN; We met at a dance in a dirigible hangar on North Island.

GROUCHO: You met him in a dirigible hangar? Was he full of hot air at the time?

GROUCHO: Ingrid Ami and Robert Crook, eh? Well, if you're a crook, you're on the right show, old boy. And you're Ingrid Ami?

WOMAN: Ingrid Ami. Yes, Groucho.

GROUCHO: Oh, well, it's the old Ami game. Are you any relation to Bon Ami?

WOMAN: No.

GROUCHO: If you were, you could clean up, you know. No soap, huh?

MAN: I was late every morning for school and finally the teacher asked me why I was late and I says, "Well there's a sign down the road says, 'School—Go Slow.' So I took my time." I didn't mind the teacher so much, it was the principle of the thing.

GROUCHO: Where did you say this happened?

MAN: In Providence, Rhode Island.

GROUCHO: Well, apparently we have very little to thank Providence for.

WOMAN: If you put the mynah bird in the cage alone and he happened to lay an egg, then you'd know that he was a lady bird. But—

GROUCHO: That doesn't mean a thing. I leave my milkman

191

alone and he leaves eggs every morning—and he's certainly no lady. And according to my cook, he's not even a gentleman.

WOMAN: (To a mynah bird) Raffles, when you heard Groucho last week, did you laugh? When you heard Groucho on TV did you laugh? Did you laugh, Raffles? *Raffles?* What are you gonna say to Groucho? What do you say? What do you say, Raffles?

GROUCHO: Can he do anything else? Here we have a bird with a human brain, and on this stool we have a human with a bird brain.

MAN: When I was at the age of fourteen I had seven men under me.

GROUCHO: Were you working in a cemetery?

GROUCHO: Miona, what were you doing in a bar? Were you playing Parcheesi?

WOMAN: No, it wasn't a bar. It was a cocktail lounge.

GROUCHO: A cocktail lounge. Well, there is a difference, you know. When you pass out in a bar you just lie there. When you pass out in a cocktail lounge they're more refined. They shove you under a table and then they kick you.

GROUCHO: How do you like marriage, Roweena?

WOMAN: Oh, it's fine. It's very, very nice.

GROUCHO: Is it all that you anticipated?

WOMAN: Oh yes, yes. And I don't have to feed the chickens. That's why.

GROUCHO: You don't feed the chickens anymore?

WOMAN: No, no. That's why.

GROUCHO: That's certainly a good reason to get married. It's certainly much easier to feed one rooster than a flock of chickens.

GROUCHO: (To a man giving him a piece of the Blarney Stone) What is this good for?

MAN: Well, it gives you the gift of gab. As a matter of fact, if you kiss it, you'll become more eloquent than you are presently, by far.

GROUCHO: When I'm reduced to kissing rocks, I'm going to cancel my subscription to *Playboy.*

WOMAN: Every woman has three ages—chronological age, a physical age, and an emotional age.

GROUCHO: That's true, isn't it, Mark? A man has seven ages and they're all lousy.

GROUCHO: How did you meet your husband?

WOMAN: He pulled up alongside me in his little white sports car and honked.

GROUCHO: What was he? A goose?

WRITER: As a matter of fact, I have a book out—*The Eternal Search.*

GROUCHO: *The Eternal Search.* Is it about a fellow looking for his car keys?

GROUCHO: When you get a flash that somebody's stranded in the snow, do you come bounding up the slopes with a keg of brandy around your neck?

MAN: No, uh, Groucho—

GROUCHO: Or do you drink it before you get there and just give him the empty keg? No, I'll tell you—you can't have your keg and eat it too.

MAN: We don't use brandy because after a shot of brandy, or after giving the patient or victim brandy, he will be colder within a half an hour than he was previous to the time that he drank the brandy. But we give him soup—

GROUCHO: After a half hour with a keg of brandy, who cares if he's cold or not?

193

WOMAN: I go to Los Angeles City College.

GROUCHO: You live in Guatemala and you go to school in Los Angeles? Aren't you a little rushed when you go home for lunch?

GROUCHO: And you're Taylor Williams, huh? You're a fine-looking man. How old are you, Taylor?

MAN: I'm sixty-seven.

GROUCHO: Sixty-seven. Oh, sort of Old Taylor, huh?

GROUCHO: What do you have to know to be a good fisherman?

MAN: Well, you have to think like a fish.

GROUCHO: You mean you have to be a chowderhead?

GROUCHO: We'll start right off with the big question. How old are you?

WOMAN: I am half Italian, half French.

GROUCHO: Well, that's a nice combination—half French, half Italian. You oughta have a lot of happy thoughts. I know a fellow who's half Scotch and half Soda, and he's happy all the time.

WOMAN: About marriage, we still have that old saying which is that women are the hind legs of the elephant.

GROUCHO: Women are the hind legs of the elephant? That's only when they're wearing slacks, isn't it?

MAN: My grandfather was in the oil business.

GROUCHO: He was in oil? Was he a sardine?

MAN: No, he delivered kerosene from house to house.

GROUCHO: You're pretty clever, aren't you. Are you married?

MAN: Yes, I'm married.

GROUCHO: Then you're not as clever as I thought you were. How did you meet your wife?

MAN: Well, I met her in the county jail, Groucho.

GROUCHO: Now you're talkin'.

GROUCHO: (To a British woman) Eileen, you have a very unusual accent. Do people in England ever comment about it?

WOMAN: Well, no, they all speak the same way there.

GROUCHO: Really! I'm surprised you can understand each other. No wonder you all drive on the wrong side of the road.

WOMAN: I first worked for Lloyd's of London.

GROUCHO: Oh, Lloyd's of London. I know them very well. As a matter of fact, I have a policy with them right now. If I'm torpedoed by a submarine at Hollywood and Vine, I get eight dollars a week for the rest of my life.

GROUCHO: Wouldn't you find it more exciting working for Elvis Presley?

WOMAN: No, I don't think so.

GROUCHO: Don't you like him?

WOMAN: You know, I've never seen him.

GROUCHO: You don't have to see him to dislike him.

GROUCHO: You're forty-four and you just got married last May?

MAN: Yes, sir.

GROUCHO: Are you sorry that you marked time for such a long period?

MAN: Well, no. I didn't exactly mark time. I've done it twice before.

GROUCHO: You weren't marking time, you were doing time.

JACK LA LANNE: I swam from Alcatraz Prison to Fisherman's Wharf in San Francisco handcuffed.

GROUCHO: Why? You crazy about fish?

JACK: Not exactly.

GROUCHO: Isn't that the way everybody leaves Alcatraz . . . handcuffed? What were you in for?

JACK: Well, I wasn't in for anything. It was just one of my birthday feats.

GROUCHO: Oh. Well, let's see the other one.

WOMAN: Well, I took philosophy in college, and I also read *The Power of Positive Thinking* by Norman Vincent Peale.

GROUCHO: Have you ever seen Norman Vincent peel?

WOMAN: No, I haven't. I missed—

GROUCHO: Well, it's very interesting. You should see it sometime.

GROUCHO: Your name is Charles Snow?

MAN: Charles Snow.

GROUCHO: How tall are you, Charlie?

MAN: Five-two.

GROUCHO: That's the first time we've ever had five feet of snow in L.A.

MAN: Well Groucho, you're a comedian . . . you tell jokes—

GROUCHO: Now wait a minute, that's debatable.

MAN:—And I'm a watchmaker and I make watches.

GROUCHO: Where'd you get the notion that I'm a comedian? If your watches are as run down as my jokes, they're beyond repair.

WOMAN: They seem to be emotionally dehydrated.

GROUCHO: That's a good phrase, isn't it, Mark? You say the young men you've met are dehydrated? Well what's wrong with that? Everything's dehydrated now. Just add a little water, stir—

GROUCHO: Oh, you're Atoun?

MAN: Huntoun.

GROUCHO: Oh, well you look out of tune.

MAN: It is an Arabic name, generally heard in Lebanon.

GROUCHO: Uh-huh. Whereabouts in Lebanon were you born?

MAN: Well, I was born in Ohio.

GROUCHO: Do you like to wrestle?

WOMAN: Uh, no!

GROUCHO: Have you done any wrestling at all?

WOMAN: No, not lately.

GROUCHO: Well, there are a number of girls that do wrestle. I was thinking of a couple of new holds I'd like to show you.

MAN: I'm a musician, Groucho. I play the bass viol.

GROUCHO: Well, you don't have to be so modest about it. You're probably not as vile as you think you are.

GROUCHO: (To a girl named June) June was always my favorite month. Usually June is followed by July, but beginning tonight, June may be followed by Groucho. Are you married?

WOMAN: Yes, I am, Groucho. I've been married a little over a year now.

GROUCHO: Oh, in that case, June will be followed by July as usual.

GROUCHO: What sort of work do you do, Ed?

MAN: I'm in the investments securities business.

GROUCHO: Investments securities?

MAN: Yes. We're Lester Ryans and Company. We're members of the New York Stock Exchange.

GROUCHO: You have a lot of Ryans in the fire?

MAN: Quite a few Ryans in the fire.

GROUCHO: You're on Wall Street, in other words.

MAN: No, we're on Hope Street. Wilshire and Hope.

GROUCHO: Eddie, everybody on Wall Street is on hope street.

GROUCHO: Where are you conducting your junk business?

MAN: I'm conducting it in Chico. Chico, California. Did you ever hear of Chico?

GROUCHO: Yes, that's one of my brothers. I always knew one of my brothers was going to wind up in a junk pile. I always thought it was going to be me. What do you call your junk pile? Is it some fancy euphemism like the Bon Ton Reclamation and Scrap Iron Corporation?

GROUCHO: George, I have a riddle for you. Do you know the best way to make a coat last?

GEORGE: No, unless the way to make a coat last is to make the trousers first.

GROUCHO: You know, you're supposed to do the commercials. I'm supposed to tell the jokes. I'm going to give you one more chance, George.

GEORGE: All right.

GROUCHO: Why is George Fenneman like a boiler on a steam engine?

GEORGE: I guess I'd better say why. Why is he like a boiler on a steam engine?

GROUCHO: I'll tell you why—because you're both fired!

GROUCHO: You know, I've been working on this show for eleven years and this is the first time a pretty girl has ever shown up in a bathing suit!

MISS OHIO: I think it's an honor, Groucho.

GROUCHO: Why didn't this happen eleven years ago when I was thirty years younger? Could you describe yourself for the benefit of the audience at home?

MISS OHIO: Can't they see me on the TV screen?

GROUCHO: The husbands can't. They've been breathing so hard they've fogged up theirs. So would you mind giving us your measurements? You can take them back later.

MISS OHIO: Thirty-five, twenty-two, thirty-seven.

GROUCHO: Let's see. Lumped all together you're ninety-four. That's the same as I am.

EGYPTIAN LADY: I've been married for thirty-one years to the same man.

GROUCHO: If he's been married for thirty-one years, he's not the same man. How did you meet him?

EGYPTIAN LADY: I was on a subway in New York.

GROUCHO: I thought you said you came from Egypt.

EGYPTIAN LADY: I was visiting my sister in New York and we were talking on the subway and he was listening.

GROUCHO: He was eavesdropping?

EGYPTIAN LADY: Yes, I had a very broad accent at the time.

GROUCHO: You still do.

EGYPTIAN LADY: I used to say "bawthroom" and things like that.

GROUCHO: Bawthroom, eh? No wonder he was intrigued. I guess he was wondering how you found a bawthroom on the subway. Say, why were you saying bawthroom to a strange man, anyway?

EGYPTIAN LADY: It wasn't bawthroom that attracted him. It was my accent.

GROUCHO: Whenever you use your accent you say "bawthroom"?

EGYPTIAN LADY: No, no. When I got off, he got off and asked me, "Where are you from?"

GROUCHO: And you said the bawthroom.

EGYPTIAN LADY: No! He said he was fascinated. Back then, someone from Egypt was a rarity. Today there are millions of us.

GROUCHO: There's too many of you to suit me.

EGYPTIAN LADY: So then he said, "May I walk you home?" I said, "Yes." He was very gentlemanly.

GROUCHO: It wasn't that. He was just looking for a bawthroom.

GROUCHO: Where are you from, Catherine?

CATHERINE: I'm from Paris.

GROUCHO: Do you have a husband?

CATHERINE: No.

GROUCHO: That's the friendliest gesture France has made since they sent Lafayette over here. How old are you, Catherine?

CATHERINE: In France, a gentleman doesn't ask a lady how old she is.

GROUCHO: Let's get two things straight. First, we're not in France, and second, I'm no gentleman. And if you want, you can put the second first. Well, you don't have to tell me your age if you don't want to.

CATHERINE: I don't mind. I'm twenty-five.

GROUCHO: If I were twenty-five I wouldn't mind either. How long have you been in this country? Have you been here long enough to meet any American men? What a question!

CATHERINE: Since I have been here, I've been very distrustful. With American men there is an angle to everything.

GROUCHO: Any man who can find angles on you ought to have his eyes examined.

CATHERINE: Nothing much has happened, Groucho. I can't find a man who can make me tingle. It's important for me to tingle.

GROUCHO: What do you mean by "tingle"? You mean like tingle, tingle little star?

CATHERINE: No, no, no! You know!

GROUCHO: No, I *used* to know, but I don't know anymore. I haven't tingled since William Jennings Bryan was running for office.

Outtakes

(WE NOW come to that section where all children should be sent out of the room: the Outtakes Section. I advise this be done for a very important reason. The saucy sallies are so tame by today's standards that our kids would hoot them down, and no telling what they'd do to us. These interchanges never got out of the studio. Here, revealed for the first time, is our secret shame.)

GROUCHO: Would you go with me to a movie if I promised to sleep all through it?

WOMAN: Yes! I'd be happy to. I'd even drive you there.

GROUCHO: You would?

WOMAN: Yes!

GROUCHO: Would you pay for the tickets?

WOMAN: No, I have a friend who owns a drive-in theater, so we would have passes.

GROUCHO: Oh, well, do you know what your neighbor looks like?

WOMAN: Oh, yes.

GROUCHO: Do you take your neighbor to the movies on her passes?

WOMAN: No, she's got a family, she stays home with them.

GROUCHO: Oh, you mean nobody that has a family goes to the movies?

WOMAN: Well, her kids . . . I don't know . . . sometimes they take her kids too, but she doesn't like to drive them. 'Cause she has a husband. And they just stay home.

GROUCHO: You mean that . . . what you're saying is that . . . what you're saying is that if you're married, you don't have to go into a drive-in theater. Is that it?

WOMAN: I guess so.

GROUCHO: I'm certainly learning a lot about the younger generation here tonight.

GROUCHO: What sort of work do you do now, Karen?

WOMAN: Alphabetically, or should I just rattle it off? Let me see now, I—

GROUCHO: I don't care, you can attack this any way you want.

WOMAN: I'm a—

GROUCHO: And later I'll do the same thing to you.

WOMAN: Promise?

GROUCHO: She may not know about Johnson being impeached, but she knows many other things. Which are far more important.

GROUCHO: Don't you think she's very attractive? She's married, you know.

MAN: Yeah, she told me.

GROUCHO: Are you married, too?

MAN: Yes, I told her.

GROUCHO: Did you tell her that immediately?

MAN: No. Afterward.

GROUCHO: Oh. After what?

MAN: After the ball. No.

GROUCHO: Well, were you after it?

GROUCHO: Well what did you do a-way up North in Tennessee, Grandma?

WOMAN: I ran a boarding house for the college students, and ah—

GROUCHO: College students?

WOMAN: Yeah. And I had the boys on the first floor and

the girls on the second floor, and it sure kept me busy. Lots of times I felt like usin' a broom.

GROUCHO: Why, did you want to fly around the room or something?

WOMAN: But then I'd come down.

GROUCHO: Well, I don't understand. Why did you have the boys on the first floor and the girls on the second floor? Seems to me you should've given the girls the fair preference and put them on the first floor.

WOMAN: Well, we didn't.

GROUCHO: You didn't, huh? You have no reason for this at all?

WOMAN: No, not especially.

GROUCHO: Well, what happened, why did you want to use the broom? Was it getting pretty filthy, this joint?

WOMAN: Well, sometimes you feel like it.

GROUCHO: Well, what was going on?

WOMAN: Just different things.

GROUCHO: I didn't know there were any different things. I'm so innocent and naive.

GROUCHO: I had never seen anybody dressed in evening clothes, except my father when he got married.

GROUCHO: What were you going to say about your car?

WOMAN: Well, when I go into a service station and the attendant comes over to check my battery, I don't let him.

GROUCHO: You don't let him check your battery?

WOMAN: No.

GROUCHO: I should say not. Anybody ever tries to check your battery, you hit 'em over the head with a wrench.

GROUCHO: You weren't even engaged and you were discussing with this fella how many children you were gonna have? Isn't that a little premature? There's many husbands been hooked by that process . . . I'd say a good fifty percent.

203

GROUCHO: Are you sure your husband hasn't lost some of his buttons in this laundry?

WOMAN: I don't think he ever lost his buttons in the laundry, but he lost his pants at the wedding.

GROUCHO: That's a little premature, isn't it?

GROUCHO: What have you learned after being twenty-five years in politics?

MAN: Well, the old-fashioned way is still the best.

Audience roars

GROUCHO: I must have some reputation, you know. There isn't anything anybody can say to me anymore that doesn't evoke some kind of a dirty laugh from the audience. What do you mean by the old-fashioned way?

GROUCHO: Now, John, are potatoes really fattening?

MAN: No, sir. It's what you put on them that's fattening.

GROUCHO: Whaddya mean?

MAN: Oh butter, cheese, but if you put that on a mattress, it'd fatten you too.

GROUCHO: That's one of the few things I've never had on a mattress.

GROUCHO: Well, in what way is your husband romantic, assuming that he is . . . which I question.

WOMAN: Oh, man, have you ever been made love to by a Frenchman?

GROUCHO: Not that I can recall. This is getting like a burlesque show. What does this Casanova look like?

WOMAN: Well, he's a little fella. He's six foot five, two hundred and fifty pounds of—

GROUCHO: Pure mush?

WOMAN: No, all man.

GROUCHO: All man, huh? What makes you think that just because a man is five inches taller than six feet that this makes him a man? You know it doesn't go by size. A man's size has nothing to do with his ability in any way. I'm trying to keep this on a euphemistic level, but I question very much whether I'm succeeding.

WOMAN: I saw a woman friend had a Mixmaster.
GROUCHO: A Mixmaster?
WOMAN: Mixmaster, yes.
GROUCHO: You mean her husband?
WOMAN: No, my friend had.
GROUCHO: Well, what do you mean? You mean her husband was confused?
WOMAN: No, to make cakes.
GROUCHO: Oh. I thought you meant he was a mixed master.
WOMAN: Anyway you call it a Mixmaster. You put your business in there and it—
Stops the show
GROUCHO: Well, here we go again.

GROUCHO: Well, it sounds like an ideal existence. What happened to your marriage?
WOMAN: Bing!
GROUCHO: Bing? You mean you ran into Crosby?

MAN: Felt has over fifty thousand commercial uses—for ladies' apparel as well as industrial uses.
GROUCHO: Well, name one specifically.
MAN: Well, automobiles couldn't run without felt. Airplanes couldn't run. Girls in California couldn't have that new look.
GROUCHO: You mean the girls couldn't run without felt? Well, a lot of them are felt, and *then* run.

WOMAN: And he got a "Dear John letter," and I read it to him.
GROUCHO: You got a "Dear John letter"?
WOMAN: Yes.
GROUCHO: Well, there's one on every floor.

WOMAN: So we got this "Dear John letter."

GROUCHO: What is a "Dear John letter"? I don't understand. Is this put out by the American Can Company? I'm back to my old dirty self tonight.

WOMAN: My mother was a very fanciful woman. There were twelve of us in the family. We have not one John, nor Frank, nor Joseph, nor Mary.

GROUCHO: You have no john? Ah, they certainly do things differently in India.

GROUCHO: Is the oxygen business pretty profitable?

WOMAN: Well, sometimes it's almost too good. He's on twenty-four-hour call.

GROUCHO: He's on twenty-four-hour call and you've got ten kids?

WOMAN: He gets home in between calls.

GROUCHO: Imagine if he had a job around the house.

General Missed Information

YOU MAY have laughed at the hundreds of dummies appearing on *You Bet Your Life* over the years. And you think you're pretty smart. Wanna bet? Your life? We play for high stakes around here, and when will the price of beef ever go down? (If you can answer that question, you're entitled to your own show.)

The following hundred questions were missed by our contestants. In fact, some of them were missed several times. For I can now reveal with some pride that *You Bet Your Life* was solely responsible for ushering in the age of ecology. We recycled missed questions, to be missed again another day, leaving the program staff free to resolve more burning questions of the day . . . to wit, "Who dealt this mess?"

Can you do better? As my grade teacher used to say, "A score of sixty-five is passing." That shows how little she knew. A score is 20.

QUESTIONS

1. In what country is Waterloo, where Napoleon met his defeat?
2. What was the name of the stone found in 1799 that helped scientists decipher hieroglyphics?
3. What cabinet post is in charge of the U.S. Coast Guard?
4. How many squares on a standard checker board?
5. What is the word, originally French, for banter or repartee?
6. What is the length between a car's front and rear axles called?
7. Where is Nantucket?
8. What is the Cornhusker State?
9. What was Francis Scott Key's profession?
10. What kind of animal is a dromedary?
11. What is myopia?
12. What was the name of King Arthur's wife?
13. What river separates Manchuria from Korea?
14. What are potables ?
15. What is Princess Grace's last name?
16. What do you call a female seal?
17. If donkeys bray, what do elephants do?
18. Who was our only bachelor President?
19. Who killed Cock Robin?
20. What is the national motto of the United States?
21. What city was buried in A.D. 79 by the eruption of Vesuvius?

22. What was the first capital of the United States under the Constitution?

23. What was the epic film about the South made by D. W. Griffith in 1915?

24. Where is Mandalay?

25. On what street is the White House located?

26. Who spread sickness and worry on the world by opening a box?

27. If soft coal is bituminous, what is hard coal?

28. What is the name of the town in Ontario, Canada, where the Dionne quintuplets were born?

29. The Stanley Cup is given in what sport?

30. Who blazed the Wilderness Trail in 1775?

31. What is the largest city in Finland?

32. Florence, Italy, is on what river?

33. What movie was it where Charles Boyer tried to drive his wife Ingrid Bergman mad?

34. Where does the film *The Sundowners* take place?

35. What is the capital of Nevada?

36. To what country do the Bahama Islands belong?

37. What is the name of the observatory whose solar times serve as the standard for the rest of the world?

38. Under the stadium of what university was the first nuclear stockpile stored?

39. Who was the male star of *Room at the Top*?

40. Who was the female Secretary of the Treasury from 1953 to 1960?

41. Who was the ringleader of the mutiny on the *Bounty*?

42. What is the name of California's only volcanic peak?

43. In what city is the League of Nations' building?

44. Who wrote "The Ballad of Barbara Fritchie"?

45. In 1814, Francis Scott Key watched the bombardment of an American fort, and was then inspired to write "The Star-Spangled Banner." What fort?

46. What is the French word for potato?

47. What food is more widely grown and consumed than any other?

48. Clark Gable won the Best Actor award in 1934. Who won as Best Actress?

49. What profession was Jacques Fath?

50. What was Hippocrates' profession?

51. What famous Norwegian's name is now synonymous with traitor?

52. What Greek poet's name now means actor?

53. In 1949, Olivia de Havilland played a rich young woman who was disillusioned by a young suitor, played by Montgomery Clift. What film?

54. What was the post held by Vincent Massey in 1960?

55. Where is Crater Lake?

56. Where is the Hall of Fame for Great Americans?

57. Only one man has ever served two nonconsecutive terms as President of the United States. What was his name?

58. During the celebrated Scopes trial, Clarence Darrow was the attorney for the defense. Who opposed him as chief prosecuting attorney?

59. What is Art Buchwald's profession?

60. In 1579, Sir Francis Drake claimed a new land for Queen Elizabeth. He named it Nova Albion. By what name is it known today?

61. What were the first words sent over the telegraph by its inventor, Samuel Morse?

62. In 1959, Mamie Eisenhower christened the first atom-powered merchant ship. What was it called?

63. Who directed the Marilyn Monroe–Clark Gable film, *The Misfits*?

64. In what country are the ruins of Stonehenge?

65. During the campaign to pass the Nineteenth Amendment, the best-known woman suffragette was a schoolteacher. Who was she?

66. Who was Tom Sawyer's sweetheart?

67. Who is Popeye's lady love?

68. What is the highest point on the African continent?

69. Who was JFK's ambassador-at-large?

70. What was the name of the knot that Alexander the Great cut?

71. Who was the Dutchman who bought Manhattan from the Indians for $24?

72. What do you call the groups of people who are paid to persuade legislators to vote for or against a bill?

73. In what state is Glacier National Park?

74. St. Louis is in Missouri. In what state is East St. Louis?

75. The Great Smokies are in two states. North Carolina is one. What is the other?

76. Who was the Polish astronomer who said that the sun is in the center of the universe?

77. In 1958, who was the man who succeeded Sherman Adams as the President's top administrative assistant?

78. Sugar Loaf Mountain is in what South American city?

79. In what city is Tempelhof Airport?

80. What do you call the right side of a ship?

81. What plants do silkworms feed on?

82. What is Bermuda grass commonly known as?

83. What is the ancient Hellespont called today?

84. In what country are the cities of Baghdad and Basra located?

85. Legend has it that the greatest of the Greek orators placed pebbles in his mouth to overcome a speech impediment. Who was he?

86. What do you call the species of weasel whose coat turns white in the winter?

87. What sign of the Zodiac is Capricorn?

88. What is the oldest university in the United States?

89. These are the four largest places in what state? Milford, Elsmere, Newark, and Dover.

90. What Russian was known as the Mad Monk?

91. Who was known as the Swedish Nightingale?

92. Who wrote *Andersonville*?

93. What kind of sauce is served on Eggs Benedict?

94. What is a podiatrist?

95. He directed *It Happened One Night*, *Mr. Deeds Goes to Town*, and *You Can't Take It with You*. He won Academy Awards for all three pictures. Who is he?

96. Who "stole a pig and away he run"?

97. What is the word, originally French, meaning clumsy or awkward?

98. Who jumped off the Brooklyn Bridge in 1888?

99. Which of the Great Lakes does not touch the state of Michigan?

100. Name the following popular song:

ANSWERS

1. Belgium
2. The Rosetta Stone
3. Secretary of the Treasury
4. 64
5. Badinage
6. Wheelbase
7. Massachusetts
8. Nebraska
9. Lawyer
10. Camel
11. Nearsightedness
12. Guinevere
13. Yalu
14. Beverages
15. Grimaldi
16. A cow
17. Trumpet
18. James Buchanan
19. The sparrow with his little arrow
20. In God We Trust
21. Pompeii
22. New York
23. *Birth of a Nation*
24. Burma
25. Pennsylvania Avenue
26. Pandora
27. Anthracite

28. Calendar
29. Ice hockey
30. Daniel Boone
31. Helsinki
32. Arno
33. *Gaslight*
34. Australia
35. Carson City
36. Great Britain
37. Greenwich
38. University of Chicago
39. Laurence Harvey
40. Ivy Baker Priest
41. Fletcher Christian
42. Mount Lassen
43. Geneva
44. John Greenleaf Whittier
45. Fort McHenry
46. Pomme de terre
47. Rice
48. Claudette Colbert
49. Dress designer
50. Doctor
51. Quisling
52. Thespian
53. *The Heiress*
54. Governor-General of Canada
55. Oregon
56. New York
57. Grover Cleveland
58. William Jennings Bryan
59. Newspaper columnist
60. California
61. What hath God wrought
62. *The Savannah*
63. John Huston
64. England

65. Susan B. Anthony
66. Becky Thatcher
67. Olive Oyl
68. Mount Kilimanjaro
69. Averill Harriman
70. The Gordian Knot
71. Peter Minuit
72. Lobbyists
73. Montana
74. Illinois
75. Tennessee
76. Copernicus
77. Wilton B. Persons
78. Rio de Janeiro
79. Berlin
80. Starboard
81. Mulberry
82. Devil grass
83. The Dardanelles
84. Iraq
85. Demosthenes
86. Ermine
87. Goat
88. Harvard
89. Delaware
90. Rasputin
91. Jenny Lind
92. MacKinlay Kantor
93. Hollandaise
94. Foot doctor
95. Frank Capra
96. Tom, the piper's son
97. Gauche
98. Steve Brodie
99. Lake Ontario
100. "Autumn Leaves"

WHO'S BURIED IN GRANT'S TOMB?

Sorry you didn't answer more. But so you won't go away empty-handed, here's a consolation question for you. If you can't answer the first one, go on to the next. If you're still drawing a blank around Question Seven, then I suggest you start all over again . . . in the first grade.

Here are the questions and, please, no help from the audience:

   1. Who's buried in Grant's Tomb?

>*BERNIE SMITH: Groucho must have asked that question a hundred times on the show. Someone pointed out that the right answer could also be Mrs. Grant, since she's also entombed there. But if you want to be literal, nobody's buried in Grant's Tomb. People are not buried in tombs, in the sense that they're planted six feet under. They are entombed above ground.*

I said, Smith, no help from the audience. Please disregard his comments and go on to the next question:

   2. What insect is flea-brained?
   3. In what sport do we use a basketball?
   4. What was the color of the old gray mare?
   5. How many bullets does a six-shooter shoot?
   6. What is the main course of the man-eating shark?
   7. What color is an orange?
   8. From what state do we get Maine lobsters?
   9. Where do Boston baked beans come from?
 10. What state has the same name as the Mississippi River?